peter among th
towring boxes /
text bites

bill bissett

talonbooks   2002

Talonbooks
P.O. Box 2076, Vancouver, British Columbia, Canada V6B 3S3
www.talonbooks.com

Typeset in Librarian and printed and bound in Canada.

First Printing: March 2002

National Library of Canada Cataloguing in Publication Data

Bissett, Bill, 1939-
  Peter among th towring boxes, text bites

  Poems.
  ISBN 0-88922-464-1

  I. Title.
PS8503.I78P47 2002   C811'.54   C2002-910066-6
PR9199.3.B45P47 2002

The publisher gratefully acknowledges the financial support of
the Canada Council for the Arts; the Government of Canada
through the Book Publishing Industry Development Program;
and the Province of British Columbia through the British
Columbia Arts Council for our publishing activities.

thanks 2 th canada council   th writrs federaysyun uv
canada   leeg uv canadian poets writrs yuunyun canada
hous london england granary books new york   th art
kollektors n th capilano college writing practices program

thanks 2 th publikaysyuns ripple effekts bc blooom bc
unarmd mn filling station alta capilano review bc writrs
forum *th ekstasee uv aprikots* publishd in full by bob cobbing
london england *i.v. reader insomn*iac paul vermeersch ont
n imp press vanderhoof bc steev clay at granarybooks new
york 4 th time n opprtunitee n th pteros galleree toronto
thanks 2 **bill roberts** composr 4 whos mewsik th following
pomes wer writtn *repo jazz aftr th first snow i was pacing*
th balustrade   kliks from nowher whn was th regatta what
evr we ar rising latin moon vera looking ovr th citee th kaktus
yeers wanting th diffrens btween brains   thats a lot uv suit
cases 4 onlee a whil text bites ium going 2 sleep now n i remem
br th time part 1 p 1 th book is in my hed voyajuur three mon
keez ar lying down sojourn th wizard uv time sequeces uv ek
stasee swimming with debussey whos text is it aneeway   th
*origin uv missing ficksyuns sum from upcumming cd **rumours***
uv hurricane with **bill roberts**

thanks 2 jena hamilton editing suggestyun on *‘eye thot i*
saw him goin down th street ’ 2 sabine campbell editing sug
gestyun on *writtn aftr his going 2 spirit place* n 2 jonathan
rainbow who insistid on saving th last line uv ths book -
‘..n dispersing agen’ n 2 rita aufrey who sd th words *‘protekt*
th gift   protekt th gift...’ n 2 maureen medved who whn i sd 2
her th words on p 24 *‘it was th day’* sd thats a pome write
xaktlee what yu just sd bill n tom graff 4 th words in *‘moon*
droppings’ ‘arriving’ n *’aestheiks’* n 2 helen macaferty 4 th
time n place 2 write *‘i was going 2 sleep’* n rampike toronto
n 2 roger maglio gear/fab records 4 reissewing awake in th
red desert inkluding 3 bonus tracks from 2001 with bill
roberts composr from ths book *‘i was going 2 sleep 1’* th
book is in yr hed n *‘meeting at th transmittrs centr’* from b
leev abul char ak trs n 2 housepress *‘th oranges uv oranta*
ngua derek beaulieu producksyun why i sing th blues arsen
al pulp editid by jan zwicky n brad cran

rwanda

rwanda

rwanda

rwanda

dragon boat   moon credit

dere reedr
dew yu remembr th storee

what is th hero weering

why is th hous
   now on bicycul wheels

its not eezee 2 stretch
  a storee line ovr 300
      yeers or pages

dew yu know how yu
     got heer

n how yu
n how yu   n how we

th watr was kleer enuff 2nite
2 beautifulee reflekt our veree
optimistik gazes toward th moon
n th sky n th fello travellrs who

waitid 4 us all on shore with
hopefulee opn arms

as we bcame closr / i cud see
wun uv our frends / arms n per
haps part uv his heart bleeding
undr his cape against th cold nite
air n thru th margins settings ths
meeting in th suddn stinking winds
i wantid 2 lay with him agen

repo jazz

dansing at th raging club
finding th beet   sparkling
rimez   no time 2 wundr
wher it all goez   it goez
hunee   hunee it goez

dont feel bleek   whn eye
cum home   speek 2 th
towring nite sky ium not
alone   speek 2 th dreem
eye carree on eye carree on

with me its not onlee in
me its above below n all
around me   thers no reelee
names words 4   bask in
th heet th ship is ths nite

dansing at th raging club
eye can cum thru bodeez fly
kik up kik up kik up hiii
in th beet hands rage up 2
th rolling sigh takes us in

takes us in   take us in biy
keep on cumming 4 mor
no time 2 wundr   why is that
no time 2 wundr   how is that
takin us in ths way n that

takin us in finding th beet
takin us in that way n ths
takin us in finding th heet
takin us in ths way n that
takin us in being   th beet

time is sew elegant

its spliced inside space
like in an old star trek episode
yu know almost a prfekt fit

like a shu or runnr tho sertinlee
like a boot at timez it wobbuls n is
2 much or not enuff it can b
just fine as well

we entr time n space   starting
out small
n thn get veree large
seeminglee n thn start 2 shrink a
lot uv erthlings dew n thn get
small agen n go

time is us   space is what wer in
until wer not a littul knowledg can b
gud 4 art theree can bcum fakt fr a
whil   arint we all deeplee deludid
sumwun dusint show 4 an apointment
what happns   we have mor time like

scallops mirakuluslee getting largr n
largr agen th squisheeness we all cum
from th womb uv th see eye uv galaktik
dna *ther* sumtimez it can help not 2
get our own way we ar kreetshurs uv un
sertintee poignansee n yernings
breething in th xhaust uv th narrativ
th xhaustid narrativs   hello

aftr th first snow

iul b standing on th shore
uv th rivr across from yu yr hous n yr time
will yu see me n bring a boat out 2 greet
me   is it reelee me
is it reelee yu

n i row with yu across th
calming watrs   th burgundee flowrs
n whisking birds sing ovr th
slite murmurings uv th watr

will we have t n smile at th
passages uv time

aftr th first snow b4 th rivr freezes
will yu cum 2 gathr me from th
othr shore n row me in2 th south
far from th mirage
uv meening

n a surprize first wintr storm
brews n hatches its frozn tentakuls
all ovr us   n th lake freezes
n th rivr freezes
n th sky runs cold
n th rhythm uv th day
encloses th fire
n th jaguar beauteez
uv th wintr nite

all ths aftr th first wintr snow
n eye stay a yeer unabul
we ar 2 get out it is reelee as if

writtn n no decisyuns ther
is no othr way a mirakul storm

n we drink t 4 manee months
  n smile deeplee abt destineez
    keep th fire going   fly at nite
                      dreem time

n all th bowls watr n air

  n all ths

   n all ths

    n all ths

    n all ths b side th
      rivr uv time

i was pacing th balustrade

n all th littul peopul with th big souls n big voices
     wer propping up th chess peesus on th infinit bord
4 a nu day   up th knight   up th pawns n sew on n on
eye got up tried singing sum nu songs i was working on
   but evreething remindid me uv him
            evreething remindid me uv him
        gone sew not long now
sum my face coverd in teers wher outside th bord way
   prhaps venus 312 in finit sky eye cant see now
     n is it a chess bord aneeway   evreewuns crying abt
         sumthing   its sew beautiful   sew mooving
     what cha gonna dew

     th chess peesus wer bcumming star clustrs
star galaxeez   th littul peopul wer bcumming giants
  eye was all bereft out th window wev all lost our frend
         we can bcum evn kindr with each othr each
      othr is   evree wher   each othr is evree wher
      b4 th asteroid cums whatevr hmmm th meeting
      nowun in recent yeers let me stay sew long with
      them   nowun 4 sew long   inside theyr
         intimate moments   i wud go backwards if
         it wud stall his journee no diffrens with that
    we ar all sent heer   ther until th timing within th

     dansing   remembr th circus remembr th promise uv
creaysyun   remembr us hugging each othr crying n
   hugging how strong how brave remembr how th
      bodee melts sew we can go thru th veils th cloth
         backdrop designd by   designd by   who

n thru th swirling milkee surf   wher we bravelee go
                              next
                              next
                              next   ohhh

10

whats th point

is animal husbandree th domestifikaysyun uv men
she askd   n just thn th carriage ovr turnd n
all th toffee n flesh n bone wishes splayd out on
th torrenshul drive way   thers no way 2 put it all
back 2gethr she sighd looking out thru th spidr
webs n frosting at them all in th dust men n
women laying ther 4 sum wun 2

cum along n tell them what 2 dew o get up she
spat at them iuv got 2 moov on thers burnt
moons in my hands   n a hungr in me that nun uv
yu cud   o nevr mind she shoutid ium going 2 th
parkway races if yu evr want 2 join me chill ther
down time
down hungr
down demons
down lust   UH   WHAAT
WHER AR TH UNIVERSALEE ACCESSIBUL DAY
CARE SPACES   GUARANTEED
MINIMUM INKUMS 4 EVREEWUN
WHER IS TH WAGE EQUITEE PARITEE JOB
SHARING
TH LONG OVRDUE TAX REFORM REINSTATEMENT
UV REEL TAXES ON WEALTHEE N CORPORAYSYUNS
PEOPUL AR DYING ON TH STREETS   HELLO

o thees feelings keep on travelling show yr
wares whil yu can she aveerd n yul stop sum wher
sum how laying back   feel th wind teer at th
door n th sky hot n daring turn in yr bellee
n yr mind   as th brain turns 2 gold 2 blu gold
2 sweet grass   2 blessing song

whethr or not yu make th journee 4 it
YU CAN FEEL IT THRU TH 4EST SHADOW LITE
th corgis nevr stop waving

th jellee   cats

anee pome cud ...'
jena hamilton

yu ask me   who ar th jellee
cats well th jellee cats live undr th front
gardn wher eye
dew tai chi in th morning
n wher we all picknick n
wher suitors uv th xcellent
mamsels upstares pleed
2 let down theyr hair
let me climb up on yr
follikule runway
n glide up 2 yr stars
veree late at nite   howevr

th jellee cats aftr its 4
them establishd 4 ths nite
at leest who is sleeping
with who or not all ovr town
xsept in th areas uv th vast
magik 4est ther is prhaps
not much shifting or evn
subtul slinking left 2
dew
n whos alone
th moistyur uv dreems
settuls ovr our beeting
hearts acceptanses
n whos with sum wun

th jellee cats hovr ovr us tho we ar all
totalee asleep   they ar hovring is
theyr reel life its theyr waking
lives   suspending

12

in th air hi above our gardn
     prhaps evreewher   above konkreet
       path wayze aerial alleez

they ar sumtimez greyish blu sumtimez
   orange n pink puffee jellee breething
   glowing flowing largr n smallr ovr n ovr
4 eight hours
              in th morning b4 we fling our
selvs   out th doors n off 2 work n stuff

      they go back down in2 th erth
wher they sleep all day until we dew
   th jellee cats at late nite tho
      floppee mucus n shape shifting
  suspend upwards on invisibul
    elastiks
             trailing along n dansing on
air rhythms agen
    laffing n playing on
       bunduls uv oxygen
         catching flowrs falling
      dropping from th tall air
  th jellee cats drink moon dew

toastid spicee tofu branches split
  from mango dreems
    banana n appul sighs
running onlee slitelee
   with th flying squirrels
  say blessing 4 our marshmallow
    lavendr soupee sleep
they watch mooveez abt jellee
     cats we cant see
they reed sumtimez all nite

jellee cat books we cant reed
jellee cat narrativs
jellee cat prayrs
jellee cat serenades
jellee cat shining choral
groups uv jellee cats
jellee cat harmoneez
we cant heer

wer sleeping   g nite

th jellee cats r transforming us possiblee
byond worree   narrativ 2 b
feeling our internal raptyurs

n whn we wake up in th morning
feeling sew fine
thats oftn bcoz th jellee cats have en
gorgd our endorphin reeleeses 2
such pleysyurs uv spine tingul
ing joyousness

thats all i know abt th jellee cats 4 now
g nite feel th beautiful dreems n th
jellee cats hovring ovr th
amayzing moonlite th galaktik
moonlite pours in2 our fragile bones
makes our hearts sing

ps   i ran in2 mistr pax   we wer both
leeving th magik hous n he sd 2 me
on th run   that th jellee cats had
startid an airlines n wer taking
trips 2 ... i cudint make out th
words we we all swept up in th sur
prizing winds

14

eye thot i saw him goin down th street

with sumwun i didint know   eye was sew fine
n happee with ths ium walking fastr eye call
out his name hes walking away from me
i go fastr mor he goez fastr he seems all sew
2gethr like he wud b whn things wer great n
he felt that loping almost swaggr but th thing
with th arms sew xcellent as well   n mooving
thru space   like evreethings xcellent

i call out his name agen   strangelee he dusint
answr keeps on going mor quiklee him n th
prson hes raging on with i gess with th traffik
sounds n evreething he hasint herd me n that my
frends whod told me heud gone 2 spirit ar playing
sum joke   its funnee yes n hes still heer in
ths world ium going fastr n fastr sew is he n th
othr guy wer running on th beech now sun bathrs

in onlee bathing suits look up at us speeding by
sand flying changes th melodee uv theyr devosyun
he n his frend race past bronzd prsons tord a
huge rock they run around its shadow ium ther
in a flash ium ther   my face up against th tall
slate bouldr theyr gone sumhow theyve gone in
2 th rock ium a bit hysterikul   wher duz th
rock leed 2   run my hands ovr th surface all
smooth n closd

it was sew great 2 see him agen n it was sew close 2 reel
life reel time n i know he went thru rock wch we can onlee
dew if wer alredee a spirit prson on a longr journee thn is
availabul 2 us heer tho its magikul enuff th voices surfing
ovr th liquid plumbr lakes reassur us in tympani n cascading
minor chords sew lush th orchestral rushes n harmoneez
n beautiful oftn n my frends wer joking not at all

15

kliks from nowher

thers a spirit in me
thats longing 2 b free
that cant find th way
no mattr what yu say

th dreems ar gone th towrs ar brokn

can i cum in
it hurts out heer
can i stay a whil
thers a pain in my hed

whers th arms uv th foam bed wraping round me

keep it in yr pants he sd 2 me
remembr yu belong 2 me uhuh
see th pyramids a cums b4 b
xsept aftr all th dragons he sd
breething fire on th hed lands

th watr can sing in my heart
if i let th blood vessels relax
let air get in 2 them eezee
n sift th salting wounds yu sd
kilometrs from nowher hunee

cum in2 th nite shade thers
no hazzard heer take me a long
th tigris n th lounging freightrs
we rock til dawn all our lites on

thers a spirit in me thats always
sew free that can always find th
way   no mattr what eye say

16

whn was th regatta whatevr

it was whn i was arriving at
th disapeering dock n my mates
had all gone i lookd up n saw
all th ships change in2 dreems

wher was th tactilitee
th flowrs uv being yes in me
all th time   all along

a storee is what time is it
a storee is what time is it
did i miss yu in th gardn
did i miss yu in th moon

th nite was full uv toxik whales
giant 3 metr long sharks
careful steering thru th rocks
quik changing streems biy

a storee is what time is it
a storee is what time is it

wer yu ther on th othr side waiting
wer yu ther on th othr side being
th serch lite catches us all in
th drowning waves passes us all

wer yu ther on th othr side waiting
wer yu ther on th othr side being

what time is it   what time is it
what time is it   what time is it

we saw all our ships change in2 dreemS

life

sew i dont know
what aneething meens
its a long storee isint it
that i dont reelee
undrstand

ther may b mor 2 it
thn anee uv us knows
sum peopul say th gods
or sum uv them have
cum 2 erth n hung
with us moovd among
all uv us th connexyuns
solid ther

othrs say theyr skeptikul
sumtimez beleeving life is
neithr eternal or beautiful
enuff 2 beer th horrors uv
what has happend n can

stars comingul in our
heds they play ther xciting
our transmittrrs n we ar
nevr big alwayze small
littul things biggr thn sparrows
n smallr thn treez mostlee tho
our feelings ar sumtimez
huge

n thos change n go down
in2 us as we grow bcum
beetul n dragon fly

evn if ther ar no gods as sum
peopul say xsept what we
dreem we can still love
4 pees n th tendr road

notes in august   /   th drum resting

peopul prhaps bravelee laff at love theyv bin around
th block or 2 or theyr fritend uv love now but its love
  that brings us home   he sd   touching me

sumtimes our fingrs can hurt from th writing uv it
  partikularlee th thumb n 4 fingr wrappd round th pen
  digresyuns on th mytholojeez uv compleysyun dreem
  its anothr nite in th tall kastul yu know now how yuv
  bin hurt in love disapointid stressd prevents yu from
  finding 2 trust that mutualitee agen th skript unkovrs
    cawsyun or on th seventh line th puzzuling enigma
  bcums kleer whats ther go blank upon th nu undr
  standing mor enriched n upliftid from th loves yuv
  xperiensd th memoreez can turn 2 bettr wuns n ium
    alredee having ther is having tho not 4 longing onlee
    th goldn blissful kontinuing present if our soshul
      guaranteez ar in place th memoreez can enhance

at sum highr levl byond narrativ ther is no
  storee reelee eye touch yu anothr he askd me
if he cud blow me i found ths whatevr n eye
  sd ium marreed 2 a veree cool guy n he sd
o fuck off n i wunderd how my sinseer remarks
  cud caus such offens   i did say thanks anee
way   wher is th beginning middul end

  what yu remembr yu let go in th undrtow
evn yu spred yr seed thru th entire pantheon
uv th star gleeming sky th inkee milkee
    ness uv th northern lites   ther ar sew manee
  wayze uv loving being   who reelee takes yu home
      tho we can count th dayze n nites uv love
                    nothing reelee adds up

voices in th air condishyuning darts uv lettrs
n journals eye was crying 2 reed a gud frend who
stayd radiant thru th loss uv his bodee heer in
    ths dimensyun erth plane shrapnel countree trew
    lace n lushyus mouths playing tamboreens brass
a moaning cello fills th air changes th spruce treez

recentlee a coupul on theyr huneemoon walking
along th surf on th shore beech at cow bay nova
    scotia bcame singul in a flash th ocean undrtow
tuk wun uv them out 2 see out big wave gone 4evr
    from heer place uv separaysyun pain joy ekstasee

2 reed agen that skript th loving ther 4 his frends us
tho ther is no hierarkee uv being highr or lowr or
    purpose letting go th self obstakuls uv disapoint
ment angst not getting stuk in anee fissures 2 long
2 welcum changing bcumming mor flexibul groovin
takes time   go with th vibe if yu can   th necklace

in th sky brillyant lites from pours n flows out
    uv from our fingrs as we danse its love he sd
that takes us home

taking off my shirt

we ar rising

we ar rising
  ovr th magik islands in2 space yu n me
  n whn its time all our frends n th festiv
  juggler was he calld life   or was that me

  we ar rising
ovr far oceans sew deep n wide all th tides
give way 2 jellee   bottoms uv our feet fly
  bath th kaktus uv th air th 4ests undr

we ar rising yu n me in2 stratospheer out uv
galaxee succulent strawbereez evreewher cummin
in2 dreemee harbor eye reech out n touch yu yr
teers entr my skin we feel mor reel

evn ghosts n spirits sing   sew warm at last
goldn yello full breething

                hope 4 nothing live within
                hope 4 nothing live within
                hope 4 nothing live within
                hope 4 nothing live within

she was kalling her
he was kalling her   she was kalling him   he was kalling
him n they wer all kalling each othr hope 2 get 2gethr soon
like th lettus in th play wer sending love lettrs 2 each othr
needing 2 b with each othr 2 feel kompleet 2 feel reel 2 feel

reel 2 feel 2 feel   2 feeellll   feeeeeeeeeeeel
as we moov closr 2gethr th shadows uv
replikaysyun swaying ar playing in th harvest mist
burst opn all ovr th sky   2 touch th poignansee uv th
realiteez uv th longings uv th thrills uv   we ar rising
yu n me we ar rising yu n me   hope 4 noth
ing live within we ar rising ovr th magik islands
in2 space yu n me n whn its time all our frends n th
festiv jugler was he calld life   or was that me

we ar rising yu n me
we ar rising yu n me
we ar rising yu n me
we ar rising yu n me

hope 4 nothing live within
hope 4 nothing live within
hope 4 nothing live within
hope 4 nothing live within

cummin in2 dreemee harbor eye reech out n
touch yu yr teers entr my skin we feel mor
reel eye reech out n touch yu

we ar rising yu n me
hope 4 nothing live within
we ar rising yu n me
hope 4 nothing live within
we ar rising yu n me
hope 4 nothing live within
we ar rising yu n me
hope 4 nothing live within
we ar rising yu n me
hope 4 nothing live within
we ar rising yu n me
hope 4 nothing live within

it was th day eye saw

in th nuspapr theyd diskoverd a

mental hospital in sum interior

part uv nova scotia patients

chaind 2 th walls n such i

decidid that was th last straw

4 me   i was gone th next day

writtn aftr his going 2 spirit place

i cudint evn remotelee rescue him   hes alredee
rescued OR it is his journee   he had askd me if
i wud get harsh with him i askd wud he want that
or wud that help 2 stop him no he sd n he did
say he wudint follow or listn evn if i wer 2 counsel
th cure if evn i cud nowun can if its a heeling
its his 2 make aftr we all shared th love sew much
him n me we wer a coupul 4 a whil as wer othrs
with him we all share th fate uv being lovd in
return by him in diffrent wayze   n his also
loving th great flash   byond funkee

ths sew loving n dailee remindr uv loving him n
taking th time 2 let go n finding sum joy 4 him in
his decisyuns his being taste th hot spoon n th
revolving moon i can taste th highr powr ther is
no cure now tho ther can b infinit heeling n uv
kours i dont know how 2 say it change yr wet socks
sew yu dont catch yr deth   dont fall in love with
a junkee or an alkoholik i will always find a way
2 sabotage th gud times he told me othr voices   how
dew yu plan ahed who yu will meet love n he was
sew sweet n brillyant heer in ths erth place

ths is sumtimes a kold mountain its 4 lerning
unlerning lessons danse in th tendr opn heartid
stars n dont kling sew that yu dont let go n follow
yr own singul journee th great goldn n murkee
wundrs full times we shared n still tho hes in spirit
now my love 4 him as i may b look 4 anothr soon 2
dance with n he was a surprize nevr needs 2 go its
just that i miss him sew

first titul - *finding joy in defeet aftr his passing*

25

latin moon

yes yu know yes yu know
yes yu know yes yu know

it was a lovlee time
such a veree fine ride

now we go sailing
ovr th hi full moon

th lost n populatid harbors
blessings in th suddn tides

carree us in2 th soulful sky
carree us in2 th soulful sky

in2 th soulful sky
in2 th soulful sky

th soulful sky
th soulful sky

sew manee harbors
sew manee times
sew manee rides
sew manee moons
sew manee tides
sew manee manee maneee

it was a beautiful time
such a fine fine ride

yes yu know yes yu know
yes yu know yes yu know
yes yu know yes yu know
yes yu know yes yu know

veras looking ovr th   sitee

it was whn i enterd th store late
that nite thru th kreekee door uv th
gaybuld awning i saw my frends splayd out
on th kountr among th lettus n asparagus
n tinnd guds or gowds eye wunderd whethr
they wer ded or as anothr frend sd onlee
shopping

veras looking ovr th sitee
veras looking ovr th town
veras looking ovr th sitee
veras looking ovr th town

yu can sit still n still travl
appuls in a dreem sequins
johneez in th straw in th staybul
meeting by th milkee galaxee

rubbing our legs 2gethr like krikits
heer is a pees uv immortalitee in ths
moment   *feel th heet n th passyun*
outside uv mesyuring time

ya kosh a mana hiyakee
ya kosh a mana hiyakee
hunee huneee

cum 2 b   cum 2 b
cum agen cum agen
cum 2 b   cum 2 b
cum agen cum agen

inside ths green goldn being
inside ths green goldn being
inside ths green goldn being

at th moon slide kafay

has ths bin dun   maybe iul get a job in a
kafay dish out bowls uv metaphysikul soup evree
day n sum interesting things 2 say jimmee sd

yu kno th kind uv grill th kind uv drill it wud b
home 2 all th seekrs coz our specees is sew whackd

n that inkludes yu n me orion dansing in th
                    mercuree falls   merci et amour from th
countree uv yes but sumtimez i know wher th
track is n calmlee abul 2 rock with evreething as it
cums up   play thru th mayze uv th world
        connekting th dots n b aware n not aware uv
we wunderd who wrote ths n   wud th   wer in th
        qwestyuning grid   in th town uv th last refrain
wher we can b in 2 spaces uv reel n refreshing
        relasting   anee qwestyun supporting 2 ask
        anee ambivalens enjoyd 4 th rimes they ar
but thats not what i was gonna say   b loving yu
evr wundr aftr pulling yr pants back on aftr
        phone sex   finishing yr packing n hedding 2 th
airport wun eye or maybe both squinting sum teers
            sigh n relees fragile vulnrabul see th buds
growing on th mountin ash jump in2 th vehikul

yes bring yr qwestyuns heer make a stab at th
present as it is 2 enjoy not onlee th happee ending
    konstrukts or blaming miasmas mix em with th
    nooduls lentils   cawleeflowrs th chickn broth
surprizes me eye cud still b konnektid nd onlee
ium responsibul 4 what i dew no have 2s or shuds
mistr coupul or sew hours a day as th moon watr
slides up th street we raise th levl uv th countr each
day til wer eeting on th ceiling n th galoshes all th
time onlee part uv th deel heer n evreewher th moon
watr rides n subsides n drops its levls we wundr

what kind uv kreetshurs ar we
can we love mor
can we share mor
can we rock mor   finding anothr twist
uv moon shard in th kidnee n been soup
wash it down it mixes sew well in th moon slide
kafay at dawn   4 a whil th tredmill
disapeers   is gone

look

th erth is heer agen 2day

we still have a home

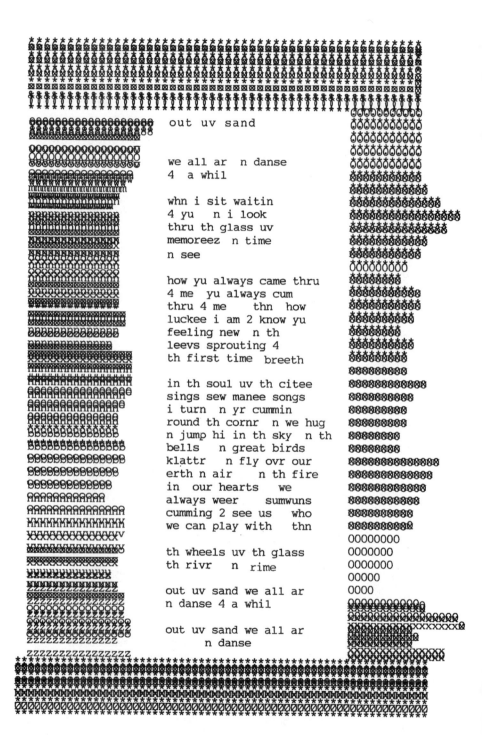

out uv sand

we all ar n danse
4 a whil

whn i sit waitin
4 yu   n i look
thru th glass uv
memoreez n time
n see

how yu always came thru
4 me yu always cum
thru 4 me   thn how
luckee i am 2 know yu
feeling new n th
leevs sprouting 4
th first time breeth

in th soul uv th citee
sings sew manee songs
i turn n yr cummin
round th cornr n we hug
n jump hi in th sky n th
bells   n great birds
klattr n fly ovr our
erth n air   n th fire
in our hearts   we
always weer   sumwuns
cumming 2 see us   who
we can play with   thn

th wheels uv th glass
th rivr   n rime

out uv sand we all ar
n danse 4 a whil

out uv sand we all ar
    n danse

30

th kaktus yeers

th medicine woman
tuk me 2 meditate on th
 kaktus   how littul watr
they need 2 keep going
she sd yet they thrive
     chek it out
        chek it out

memoreez uv trew loves
great adventurs brokn promises
   great greef also remembring
what she showd me in th
kaktus green hous anothr novembr
cumming in thn cold blustree
still a chance 2 find tropikul
paradise n sum wun 2 love b4
wintr sets in   b4 wintr sets in

ths littul watr 2 keep on from
falling thru turquois nets uv stars
   th warm love maybe wintr storm
soon th face in th glass framed by
 icikuls th camera draws back
     farthr n farthr away
        farthr n farthr away

sumtimes it helps not 2 get yr own
way looking out thru th tapestreed
air la neige encore la neige encore
falling on n covring our roofs n
windos n th beautiful kaktus yeers
spring n summr souls etchd by
   snow drifts n ice etchd by
      snow drifts n ice

31

wanting

wanting n wanting n wanting n wanting n tin
wanting n anting n nting n ting n ing n n n ti
g g g an w w ting wan tin g g tingA wn wn
wanting wanting n w w a a n n t t i n g

b4 time ther was sew much n aftr a time ther is
  sew much wanting wanting wanting
      g g g   wanting n wanting
   w w   w w   wanting   n   wanting
     a a   A   wanting   n   wanting
   ant t t t   wanting n wanting   sew
 n not wanting
 n not wanting   how is ths sew diffrent
  aw awa   awa   aw ww www aaa   wuhhh

wher was that line eye put it in th salmon
              DRAWR

ium looking 4 th beginning uv time wher evree
       thing rimez   wher nothing rimes
                wher nothing rimes

b b b b breth heetr tr b b e h ethr br br eeth
      bet th bet th bet th

murmurings uv lettrs korrespondences   undr th
karpeting pet th kars love th fossil fuels admire
n karress th hacking butanositeez th gasping 4
       striving 4
          b r e t h

go in2 a bar

in th countree go up 2 th bar
ask 4 tonik watr xcellent n a
guy a bit grizzuld next 2 me
sz yu lookin 4 sum littul gal 2
get next 2 2nite

well no i sd ium not

yu arint wun uv them panseez
ar yu

well yes i am as a mattr uv
fakt i sd not sure abt th flowr
but th intensyuns

well ths place isint 4 yu bud
yuv made a big mistake he sd

i finishd my drink put it
down on th bar

i sd i thot ths was a publik
place i gess not

left thinking glad he cant
get in2 our places

glad we have sum places

ther is sew much plentee

jet lag fhoning home
  paintings selling well its a
  dry wind 2nite   purpul
  berree nite   voices rising up
  in2 th pervasiv mist a littul
  protesting   i cant see like
  ths swiming thu air cant see

    as if we cud change anee
  uv th wethr   desires
  whn we dont try 2 kontrol
  kontrol mor can happn
  n balans onlee our
  selvs not th othr

  sir wheedul on th beepr
  wait 4 th star filld skies
  wait 4 th dreems 2
      realize   WHAT   i sdi
    dont want 2 wait o no
  why cant it all b happning
    now   i miss my frends
    back home   zatria

    its a wheel n a turning vespera
  mor jet lag sum wundr rearrange
  all th furnitur put up th set its
  cool now   its hand touching
  sparks uv sum honestee in th

  brig in th laundree room we
  meet whil falling in2 th washr a
  round th time uv fast spin othr
  side uv th street in2 th gardns way
  b4 closing time we flash o its
    sew great wer we made 4 each
  othr evn its hell on our spines

aneeway we dont *have* peopul
theyr thinking it ovr or not my
beleefs ar4 me not 4 aneewun els
2 comply with   ium not being man
ipulatid by aneewun

agen wheels n circuls n what
mattr xsept 2 b kind n not second 2
aneewun   no wun is bettr thn
anee wun   els

hearts in th snow storm in th sand
blizzards still leeping on like th fish
we sumtimes ar in th wall   in th
restaurant at port stanlee   moov
ing theyr lips tord us greeting
bubbul words translating us

our time is heer   th peopul cumming
in from th watr all bronzd n aura shining
off theyr bodeez thik thighs watr
peopul cumming in2 shore
from sum far off n vast watr place
ther was a breez ther we can see that
on theyr bodeez theyr mouths mooving
like th fish in th wall sum reel air also
prhaps not like heer wher th air is imitay
syun look at us puzzuld as they walk on
th sand   we have clothes on ar passd out
from th heet   wev left our fins at home   we
sit n talk talk abt th politiks heer
on erth th censoring kontrols

why duz th ruling klass want 2 rule
aneeway why duz aneewun ar we luckee
we ar onlee pesants can still have sum
passyun   sum idea talking among each othr
keeping it up   th konspiraseez against freedom th
liquid air heer by lake eeree starts 2 cool us evn
in ths blistring closing heet

weesuls
we can get adult hold
    grudges fall in love with th
      furnitur   soonr or latr we
    have jiltid n bin jiltid

    th ordr n th sequens
    dusint mattr much mistr ms
  martyr she sd eye dont know he
  sd   thats a littul 2 absolute isint
    it hmmmm maybe she sd

    th emerald qween talking
  with th raven man prins

  its still up 2 us 2 b happee n not
  embroidr sum losing emblem sum tireless
  heart ache that in xtreems uv heet or
    cold mite finish us off like alls fair in love
 n war he askd n why turn possibul love in2
  troubul love changes we moov on can keep
 going its not 2 settul th dust it dusint th
      sand at leest was veree gud in th pickshur
  eye found thees sheets at th bottom uv a
    vast pile uv papr ar thees th words yu wantid
 i have no idea uv th ordring sequins why
   weesuls aftr th first sheet is it at all what yu
 wer looking 4 will thees words fit   tho it did

    get in2 our eyez throats we cant change
      aneewun   accept theyr diffring
 opinyun uv life us   it dusint much mattr
      aneeway feel fine ourselvs say if we
    didint hurt thn theyr angr is theyr own
      dont judg it tho its all mor fluid thn that
    look how thees fish stare in2 our brains
      what dew they see ther

th diffrens btween brains

'...speeking uv dormant vokabulareez wev bin around
milyuns uv yeers yet writing didint evolv til maybe six
thousand yeers ago less thn what was th hold up was
writing not konsiderd interesting enuff or had our brains
not yet evolvd 2 accomodate th detail uv th xplikaysyuns
bareing in mind thats 2 yets o yu great digestiv systems
was it th brain wasint redee..' osten chenko in a recent
address 2 assemblee uv parshul otishans in that terribul
wintr whn th chickn was sew bad in kiev

cant find th genre entrans boxes inside boxes turtuls ovr
awning fulikalee as bestos evree nite th see cums in like
ths turbulent n veree erratik th ocean changes rhythms
n i cant help thinking uv how we writhd 2gethr on th
blankits next 2 th roaring fire it was way past th agrikult
ural revolushyun just as whn th way he moovd thru th
diaphanous curtins n yu know we bcame turgid aftr all
th wind wash whats his phone numbr on venus he askd
try his cell oh yeh

lap breks at th villa onika th pleysyurs uv reinkarnativ
                                        urgenseez
i sd i havint much time but i wantid 2 cum back they
didint give me much space 4 ths in th transformativ
                                                module

referenses 2 unknown agenseez

xcellent what can we dew now 2gethr whil thers time

is ther a count onn othing in th arena

oftn its not eezee pulling yrself a
way from th banquet its not

eezee 2 evr have enuff reelee
uv th lafftr th tastes th love making
onlee sumtimes natur arranges th
withdrawl slowlee

ask th count he has storeez 2 tell uv appetites n
                              thwartid wisdoms

by th ironeez at leest uv sir madam cumstances n
th changing velositeez timing n koinsidens uv yr
heart sew

hot n suddnlee thers nowun ther all eetn up by
formalisms n big konstrukts n std's yu go out
looking 2 find th fish in th see

ask th count th maintenens uv th
kastul alone th space 2 b it
always ther is no or sew oftn can
we use sumthing mor or less

try ths can yu remembr sexual
caring admiring th curv uv
his back as yu guide him in2
yr mouth 2day i can n dew yr

cum tastes sew gud i say 2 him
thank yu he sz as we merg in
th aurik beem in th tapestreed lobbee
in barcelona n brokoli swimming in
my gayze as he enterd thru th veree
diaphanous curtins th redee surf
rolling on2 th sand below is it
all deskripsyun i wonderd th
raining car surrendrs 2 our
summr heart song evn th snow
is soon deeplee falling *count*

count onn othing opns th door 4 me as eye
leev th place uv ekstasee n pass sum frends
from th group therapee on erth say loving hello
they happend 2 b ther as he hapend 2 b ther
as eye did happn 2 b ther n th flowing out in 2 a
lite spritzing n a bit uv snow swirling soon n th
evning sun darkning in th neon opaque th count
smiling closes th door aftr me as i got out in2
th lizard nite air sz thank yu eye beem hed beem
bodee stir on going letting th air breth in2 it

ther was a pain in me th count latr konfidid 2 me
each day it was in a diffrent place   wun day in my
hed anothr in my back bellee leg etsetera   th
pain wantid 2 get out each day i meditatid
did tai chi   it was a bounsing ball ths pain all
wayze returnd sum wher els tho i kept at thees
devoysyuns n visiting gud wizards it went th
pain evenshulee n flew off in2 th

gold bird in th purpul sky rushd off with th
pain in its throat transforming it in2 a sweet n
circular 4evr soundng song th sound

alerts us n distrakts us from our terribul
planning ths song uv th goldn bird n carreez
byond th purpul sky evn 2 all ears waiting
reseeving   th kount konfidid in me
ths song uv th gold bird

it was bcumming morning
n i herd th song sweep ovr th offis
towrs th eklektik neon dimming anothr days
arriving th count putting his arm around
me saying *listn*
listn
listn mor

thats a lot uv suitcases 4 onlee a whil

ium
sittin heer
all alone uv kours
n cud i wundr
wher yu went
wher yu ar
wher yu got 2   nobodee knoes   time moovs
as slow as sand up a hill

ium
sittin heer n
th barge moovs slowr
thn hope down
th watr way in
2 th harbor

ium layin heer
n th dreems cascade
sew funnee with
yu on th othr side
on th othr side

in th dreem
in ths town
thees tracks on
my mind
funnee how yu
sd it o didint
i tell yu ium
leevin 4
a whil   eezee street nevr cums not
heer not on ths erth

o didint i
tell yu ium
  leevin 4 a whil
    no i sd i
  dont recall yu
sayin that what a
  ball ths is i herd   time moovs
    yu say   as slow as
  i dont know   sand up
how things change   a hill
thats a lot uv
  suitcases
  4 onlee a
    whil

  is it i
lookd at sum   o didint i tell yu
wun 2 long   o didint i tell yu
undr th willow   o didint i *tell yu*
  thats a lot uv
  suitcases 4
    onlee a whil

  embrace th moon
hug th dreem embrace   eezee street
    th long street   nevr cums not
  with no wun on it   on ths erth
        huh   not heer

    thats a lot
uv suitcases
4 onlee a
  whil

  o didint i tell yu

41

dew yu want 2 b

calm at last

in an xcellent koffin

thn they push yu in2
th fire yr frends

teers streeming down
theyr faces

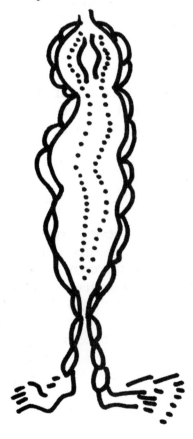
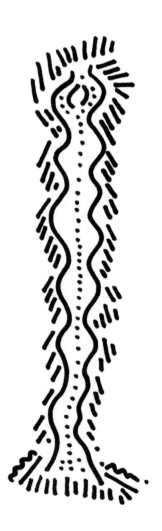

text   bites

just yu just me   just thee   just evreewun is   ar
th trewths uv th text   its margins   n infiniteez

th taktilitee uv th text carvd in our brains minds souls
duz th text ground yu   round yu me

th turbulens uv th text its focus n disarray   sway

th tempestuousness uv th text   th tortur uv th text
th storee lines uv th text relentless trewisms n realisms
th hypnoses uv th text its trajektoreez intr textualis

th torment uv th text   th terror uv th text   no

th tremor uv th text   th roar uv th text   uhuh

th ovrwhelming tango uv th text uv th text uv th text

sub th teeses uv th text   th eez uv th text   th
tautolojee uv th text   th loosness   its lostness yes
kon   text   ex   t   t   see u a l

th x t   uv th text   textual vishyun vishyn xpanding

wrestuling with th text   has th text got yu down is it
enscribing yu uplifting yu   mooving yu enkripting yu
enrapturing yu   imprinting yu   th taming uv th text

th candour uv th text its ardor armour amour and or
th testimoneez uv th text its lies n loopholes omisyuns
testes moneez its storeez loop d loop pooling poling
polling th xtent   uv th   text   o text me   text me
                                        on sum

                        regular basis

turquois n silvr

4 **pk page** whos writing
inspird thees images
thredding

poetree lifts me   we rise 2 th
kontinuum we ar thredid 2
parts speks uv onlee parts uv
speech prhaps b4 result drivn uses uv
langwages uttrances wer vowell kon
stonant stakkato flowing toys in th
air btween peopul kon sta ta ta kon on
on well on a tin vo tin uum   um mu look
up thers a meteor we ar all falling stars
words wands ords   bubul baubuls

sliding thru th kaleidoscope mirroring
heers a view look at that us leek
ing wun aspekt onlee uv infinitee
n changing we ar inside th
endless shiftings rods
amethist topaz turquois th
diamonds uv th radians
uv being n soshul
konsciens precisyun n
clariteez uv undrstandings standing undr
gliding n dansing 2gethr
inside th 17 kilometr hi oxygen
veil cloud silvree breth home 4 us
molekular transparenseez

we breeth n ride thru

eye discoverd yu waiting 4
me in th 1/2
dark our courting

44

went on like ths 4 manee
yeers

latr it cud seem like
an eye blink endlesslee
wuns beem uv glowing each
time we brout our
flash lites n canareez 2

i can keep going 4 sure
what they heer on erth call
sumwuns knocking

remembring yu inside my
wing as we take off   n sail

thru
th kaleidoscope we ar inside uv
sparkling amethists topaz
turquois diamonds
prayrs 4 flying n

xcellent wundr timez   will we meet
agen outside uv infinitee memoree
time bunduld inside us n th
bird

lipsucksyun redress

                    on rainee seesyun dayze eye sumtimez
sleep metaphorikalee undr th bed or on a veree
long leef barnakul green n drink endlesslee th still living
stars onlee b vulnrabul 2 th nameless god godess within
 not 2 th binaree propaganda valus certinlee kontradik
toree n will probablee finish our specees off our survival
instrumentaysyun cant get in 2 close n aneeway we arint
 sure we cant know tho we know abt fossil fuels dioxins
 all th pollutants n theyr xistens in relaysyun 2 hierark
ikul socio ekonomik strukshurs sew thers a huge snow
falling 2day its veree beautiful profound changes in soshul
strukshurs ar taking place eye had a dreem in three yeers
 th rite wing who ar ruining our lives sd they had bin wrong
wer ms mistr takn   theyr ideolojee devastatinglee inapprop
riate   they bgan immediatelee 2 reinstate evreething theyd
 takn away   watch 4 it   summr shiftings occur in th heet
uv our loving hearts th rite wing also re desidid that
     kultural pluralism veree kool reinstatement uv evree
 thing xcellent as what can we dew abt who we ar n why
wud we want 2 sew now that evreething was okay agen n
  we didint have 2 have wun big umbrella identitee ovr us
 all we cud rage touch punishing xploitativ not cool love
  cool whn we ar alredee with th nameless ecstasee within
th mirakul uv our independens from th general ooz n mush
  we can danse out uv return 2 turn in 2 turning in yu n
me raging ovr th roof tops sliding thru th clouds maybe ther
is no god or goddess per say n we ar aneeway creatid by sum
  things up regardless uv what we beleev with being creatid
ystrday eye undrstood evreething saw felt th beautee n thn
    th fleeting thing veree cool well 4 a milisecund i was ther
  xcellent dripping our mukous membrane   sliding thru lub
rikating our watr zooping hands off pushing aneewun els
  accept th inside uv yu ther is sumwun ther alwayze at
  home not 2 b vulnrabul 2 anothr or b wanting them ther
  thers a reesyun 4 yu 2 b sleeping alone all th mirakuls ar on
th run not letting them have th powr 2 dismiss yu bullshit yu
th cars softlee slushing thr luxuree uv we soon cant afford 4

th damage dun 2 th breething skin environment
hmmm eye sd eye think i get it at first eye thot
living byond th kollektiv konstrukts   not beleeving
 th offishul storeez yes   being gud not wanting
   2 hurt aneewun n not wanting 2 b hurt duz
 ths cum from teechings implant working 4 equalitee
  th state propaganda reinforces th hierarkee jetsum
n t trickul no glimmr at th bottom uv th pond rubbr sludge
oil gas shit no antibiotiks 4boil evreething helpful stretch
 yr tits 2 th max n byond transformativ enerjeez n as zero
was saying eet ths did yu xpekt immortalitee on yr tirading
yr blaming th bizness uv accountabilitee bizness uv letting
go covr 4 yr own insecuriteez spredding rippuling effektora
pool uv all ths wud leed 2 prsonal freedom n it duz onlee
eye wantid my love 2 stay

     thn being led 2 empteeness what
drama 2 watch i had remoovd myself sew few peopul wer
 ther or willing 2 talk abt that it was whos on top etsetera
how 2 get free uv th empire thn prsonal filling memoreez
pie crusts lemon merang chek date rhubarb raisin peer
 dreems maybee i cant fix aneething 2 much maybe my
                  self n th bathing wheels i can
                  jump in2 hmmmm

ium going 2 sleep now n i remembr th time
part 1

eye answerd an ad i met him in a tim hortons he tuk me 2 his
place in his veree sleek chrysler we drove in2 th undrground
parking he usd his identi card onlee sticking it in a masheen
that loomd ovr th drive way veree neer th great marbul doors
if it wud b raining or snowing veree hard he onlee had 2 prop
it up against th inside wind shield n th masheen like a giraffe
wud bend ovr 2 klik itself against th card thru th glass 2 verify it
n also photo ideed th prson holding th card not much cud reelee get
past it he xplaind 2 me n we slid our way down th ramp down
 bathd in glistning neon secresee he was squeezing my leg tightlee
 as he spoke thees words xhaling a numbr we wer sharing
it was 4 me a welkum touch   cumming softlee 2 a stop a veree
klassee ride all my memoreez uv sex n love in cars ovr th yeers we
wer berthd in konkreet n steel far undr th erth away from th late
july above ground xcessiv humiditee koold by th soothing air con
dishyuning onlee in sum places in othr places yu cud not moov it
was a wundrful feeling whn he put his hand on my leg   was
veree cool wer heer he sd we got out n all th doors kliking lockd
tite as we left th vehikul n made our way 2 anothr door wch was
an elevator that zoomd us i wud gess anothr 5 floors down in 2 th
        embraysing n cool erth   was it waiting 4 us was it reelee
        opning its arms 2 us   duz erth have feelings certinlee wev
        hurt erth just abt enuff prhaps mor thn erth can handul
with our addicksyun 2 fosil fuels n our needs 2 hurt n destroy
        th ego uv our theokraseez alone can send us 2 obliviun we
        cant b kontent 4 long with love need inkreesd sway whatevr
        varietee fine ego a strangr fuck fine ego a littul bit can b
xcellent 4 survival n religyun ego fine spiritualitee langwages sew
        beautiful ther was no answr aneemor 2 thees luvlee qwest
        yuns that bcame th answr no answr thos uv us who cud
        wer apparentlee hedding undrground b4 th konflagraysyun
        above gets wors certinlee th othrs whn we kompleetid our
        descent as littul at first as we saw uv them wer totalee redee
        4 us th aroma uv incens n freshlee baked salmon n rice n
curree was testimonee 2 that as wer theyr opn arms filld with
        trays uv partee favors   no ths was not sumwher harshlee
        sinistr sum wher 2 obleek 2 xpektaysyuns yet it was
        secreetid obviouslee n i wud soon find out th reesons

48

dialogia that plays in th uppr brain n seers itself out b4 yu can
record it or re code it is it gone whatevr kleeranses releesing from
evn ideaysyunal ko dependenseez langwages is it all abt what
premis permitting circular inundating encirculing   th pretexts
uv opning beings sew multipul ther is no meening n ther is ar
anguling 4 time n konsciousness allowing th othr ther is nun is
espeshulee whn things ar going well duck konstrukts in kollisyun
brain ahh flowr animal not need circutree b need is ar all
redee going 4 is nevr satisfied as in full is onlee satiaysyun un
knowing hungrs knawing know posisyuns xplode intr textualis
reverens n play rage tickr taping flooding th road maps uv th
innr circutree along th tree wall its soft n sponjee ther great
thers room 4 mor always tho ther is no alwayze what happend b4

hmmm dont know abt anee always eye sd we live inside langwage
n we dont moov around it outside uv it non verbalee cumming
2gethr clasping each othr rocking off its a big planet well 2 us
aneeway memoreez kliking th doors unkliking not assessing
raging birds fly out uv our heds on our shouldrs yes its a summr
manse n th evanescent ethr uv th green prfuming erlee evning
breething sun sew hot 2day ambulances meteors cumming torn
ados splitting treez hairs we cant reelee b upset by sum wuns
behaviour tord us if our aurik shield is strong enuff theyr powr
ovr us   they dont have that how far wud we take that we ask
ourselvs reelee is it euphanism letting go uv our egos 2 not
mind pay no re entree uv suprstisyun   n yes if they cant help
it n if they reelee have no powr ovr yu how can they make yu
feel things cudint they brek out in song mor without sew much
purpos its sew problemateek sumtimes tho yu want 2 go from
wher they can find yu evn if ther is alredee no separaysyun
wud yu not avoid sumwun who was trying 2 hurt yu or kill yu
isint that an othr 2 th xtent yu want 2 b not wher they can
get 2 yu evr   yes yu 4give wud yu want 2 4get whn theyr un
relenting tord yu manipulativ hurting skuzzing attacking its
a terribul lost stuk place that puts yu in until yu aim 2 find
yr own soshul n private places yr own life wher its acceptid fine
is ths th paranoid introspektiv seksyun wheww eye almost lost
th present eye was am in n isint that wher we mostlee live can b
in th present hmmm ium not a totalee free being condishyuns
all th processes uv letting go uv th ms mistr undrstood tapes n
confusyuns n evreewun seez evreething diffrentlee yu can   turn
ing round without looking or huuh turning 2 see yu

they cant help it ther is no they its a terribul tunnul
affekts yr free being onlee if yu let it it dusint have 2
yu can stay in th kleering th radians dont let them
make yu feel guiltee thn thers a rapprochement thn
  theyul b in 2 th frenzee accusing encore thers noth
ing 2 b mad abt heer yu kant dew aneething abt them
yu can dew lots abt yrself thers 5 bilyun peopul in th
  world whn yu first startid going 2 group 2 talk abt
   how they wer ruining yr life yu realize slowlee ths
is 2 weird that konstrukt heer yu can b responsibul
4 yr own life happeeness dont need th ko dependenseez
now yr talking abt how 2 b happee yrself yu can help
  yr self help yrself yes thers lots mor on th tray n
   from wher they came from yes if it takes rewriting
yr valus memorees approaches fine if it takes re
wiring fine whatevr yu can dew it b yrself selvs no
  mattr how plural un what fleshee fleetingness by
th time i went was takn 2 th undrground places ther
  wer ar ovr 20 bilyun peopul above ground ar they
all being servd we ar all heer on such slendr threds
isint it veree ideelistik that no wun can make us feel
    sum thing   we ar all psychikalee mowd down by life

in manee othr wayze hung on on2 useless strife ther
  is no lasting empire tho ther alwayze is at leest wun
no immortalitee tho each moment is can b in ths life
a nu medievalism has engorgd th konsciousness uv th
above ground kulturs evreewher almost evreewun has
nun or sum kompewtr access nu feers nu rules nu
evay syuns nu risks nu tyraneez suprstisyuns funda
men talisms superioriteez etsetera nu povrteez veree
few peopul having enuff 2 eet adequate living kondish
yuns certain adjustmentz wer nevr made re unemploy
ment creatid from nu technolojee diseeses compewtrs n
 roboteeks eliminating jobs unrelentinglee peopul need
work n love now eithr was veree hard 2 find whn they
cant xperiens thos fritening stuff sets in chaos as in
damaging desperaysyun killing tiny ruling klasses
veree welthee huge growing undrklass blaming abounds

inkrediblee poor state run stasis govrnment working 4 biz
ness th govrnment is kind dusint like 2 cut back its 4 th
futur gen eraysyuns that th poor must b hit now 4 theyr
own gud sew they can b alrite latr thers bin far 2 much
spending revenus down cuts ar inevitabul if th rulrs ar cut
jobs will suffr is that a thret poor peopul will rise 2 ths time
uv nu giving 2 improov life 4 evreewun kindlee ordr with a
killing hand thats above ground not heer wher wer entring
is ths a think tank 4 th futur a drug running hackrs domain
   wud ther b strong kult ovrtones sew tenor his name reelee
was th maitre d uv ths place n th host guide tuk me thru
   velveetee tones veree reassuringlee   we ar all reelee alone
silkee air waves stiltid inventing we saw th laundree rooms
th flotilla uv flowr gardns n watr wayze 4 th boats motor n
sail   ther wer winds undrground n ovr a weird yet spektak
ular docking mechanism like a starlit moat we enterd agen
moist moon motor alwayze entring whn wud we b ther whr
wud ther b n what hmmmm all thots being equal ther wer
huge birds iud nevr seen b4 above ground wer they alwayze
heer flew in thru side tunnul doors wer first born heer wud
eye find out in time prehisher storeek merging seegulls n
trinaree daktuls they seemd sinseer n frendlee enuff a bit
piersing theyr gayze not bothrsum they wer veree blu fluffee
   oftn they lookd like they wer smiling at us iud nevr seen
   birds look at peopul sew much theyr pink eyez yello
   parrot eyebrows waving nowun is alone isint at leest
   sumwun inside us bside us feel th invisibul being

   we came upon a huge ballroom me in sum considr
   abul n sustaining wundr trying not 2 have my mouth
   alwayze opn we swept along on th crystal waxing floor
   sew smoothlee maybe a thousand peopul wer dansing
   raging radio hed hole morrisey t partee moist seal
   boyze 2 alanis ths was a speshul nostalgia konsert a
   90s nite kool we dansd 4 a whil my guide n me n
   our maitre d veree rocking we cud see th full moon
   thru a beautiful window uv th nite sky above ravens n
   terra minnows flying thru turquois clouds around th
   moon ths window was creatid by a sereez uv reflekt
   ing mirrors veree konvinsing well it was reel sum wher 2
   sum wun   kazillyuns uv hors hairs wer undr th parkay
   danse floor bords making th dansing veree buoyant n
   totalee wundrful eez thru th rockin moovments

anothr huge room   that sumwun is whatevr plotting 2 hurt
   yu whatevr is no reeson 4 not ackshulizing yr own life get it
   th hallway btween coatid in ceiling 2 floor collages uv old nus
papr klippings things events that wer huge in th outtr direktid
   worlds uv long ago faces that attraktid with great lightning th
worshipful gayzes uv milyuns now old nus isint it strange lost
gods n godesses wher ar theyr worshipprs dew thees gods miss
   us or can they catch up on sum reeding they alwayze wantid 2
dew ar th neurona uv adulaysyun alwayze in place n rekovrabul
by th objekt subjekt transferens is it still ther in th airwaves
   say like a great scene uv enkountr n significans submisyun
yielding 2 mutual penetraysyun enkountr scene wher ar th
   kountrs arint they 4 scrubbing cutting vegeez sumtimes in
th morning can yu stop eeting filets in2 shaping 4 baking
boiling displaying magazeens dry goods in store eye need
sum wet guds 4 sure soon iul b back eye return in seksyuns
4 writing ovrdraft prmissyuns in banks how is ths with a prsons
legs toez genitals hair mouth fingring tits eyez bellee button
gleeming in th crescent whn yu meet a sibling dew yu flash hey
we wer in th same womb prhaps not at th same time we wer
   tho ther in th same womb thats deep moon umbilikul thred
ding shine ovr th hay th barn yard cottages see rocks shattr
ing th eeree calm uv th nite winds ar krashing on 2 th
      glistning with see shells star jellee fish mouths opning evree
wher taking evreething in sucking sew deep all th files
merging or if they dont fine eye dont care i got my meel heer
undr th sheltr uv th wrens singing nestings on th 4 cornrs
      uv th tempul   alwayze seeming 2 b rising above th tall
kliff wher if th villagers ar happee enuff it is sd lovrs no longr
throw themselvs off in 2 th jagged craggee splintring rocks below
      thos nites uv promises yr th best n eye want yu with me all
   wayze sexual ekstaseez   joining evree limb n feetshur with
         each othr   skin sucking kissing mothballs in our pores
releez us totalee agen 4 anothr ventur   tapes n storeez releesd
   not piling up   go   in2 th endless void nevr filling th holes
filling each othr tho   2 ovrflowing cumming n cumming agen
   stickee dreeming reel sew hot thees nites by th see   we cud
eet each othr totalee   swallo each othr whol live with us 4
evr who gave us that tape we try 2 recreate   how we bcum
kindr wev bin lovd n have lovd thees lives 4evr in our skin

huge almost slave faktoreez opning up in th hintrlands
uv china india wherevr almost unmapabul places
xist n ancient affordabul lives supplantid by techno
povrtee bad watr stores wher ther was genial xchAnge
no wun wanting without supply thees disastrs put
2gethr by world leedrs from northern hemispheers not
ablee a formr prime ministr from canada now nevr
abul 2 not generalize globalize organ alley india
north am hospitals   restrukshuring th organ delivree
china dissident organs apeering inside othrs at th
top uv kours did yu see *brazil* manee yeers ago whats
nu lost childrn in south am organ farms shippd in cages
th arktik ruind by nukleer testing fightr planes
no farming 2 touch 2 pleez formr pm sz we will
adjust its temporaree nu old age peopul sz ther is no
pain fine   can we rise above our disapointments in
love nu tapes by saying love is not teritoree i wudint
aneemor act on anee emoshyunal klaim uv anee kind
ium alredee takn from not being takn ahh th kokoon
ing n th kottage industreez wanting tendr temporay
brashlee bold pull yu down n inside yu go all th way
theyr eyez look upon us in ths moovee star publik figur
old nus hall bit uv air brushing heer n ther a lot uv
peopul need ths keeps them from getting meen tho
certinlee not   alwayze idol a tree they didint theyr
almost gone now   above ground   we walk thru th
natur room now see immens images uv treez valleez
mountains medos skies birds tigers elephants all th xtinkt
tresyurs uv previous millenia   how wev evolvd sins leeving th
caves th huts th watr hovels wer we reelee onlee wun cell n
amphibious whn past recovree in our brains or anee analysis tho
cud we reelee 4get if we wer ther prhaps moovments we can
reinkarnate in a post modern ballet th dansing it is what it is
i will mourn no mor abt that loss aneeway is it reelee parts uv
wun gone   th illushyuns uv permanens   how we lovd theyr
images n natur 2 how b4 we lernd 2 evolv furthr n furthr ovr
millenia n millenia we alwayze wantid 2 teer down what weud
built up   how we bcame reelee diffrent from that rathr 2 late
nd it isint what yu remembr anee uv that can yu eet memoreez
its yr own madness n serenitee if yu need 2 remembr at all
messages cum on a sew far non empirikul thot spirit wave
n reelee rich us pouring on sum mor watr on th gardn uv
our spiritual dreems remembr we prhaps usd 2 b dragons

yu know

abt th previouslee
hapless prson who
workd 4 a long time
in th diamond xchange
in sierra leone
4 a long time what we
call on erth say ovr
30 yeers

ovr 30 yeers

evree few dayze he was
pocketing a tiny
diamond on th
assemblee line
separating th dia
monds from th
shinee gravl

n taking them home
aftr 30 yeers or sew
he left quietlee unobtrusivlee
had nevr reelee spokn
much 2 aneewun ths
was seen as a sign uv
trust

he thn in th most
undrstatid way
went 2 de beers in
england cashd them
all in say wun huge bag
uv diamonds

wun huge bag uv diamonds

he quietlee thn flew
2 madrid n livd
4evr in a kastul
ovr looking th el
grecos in th prado
wch he went 2 view
            evree day

   he livd a reflektiv
life   he did partee
wuns a month at
fashyunabul art charitee
   events   uv kours his
present name was un
recognizablee diffrent
   thn b4 eithr in sierra
leone or britin

n he was happee no   undr th spanish stars
  wun cud tell that   4evr
  or remembr him evr
    from thees hi end events   ther is wun kastul
yet he was ther   eye know uv in
2 b reveeld as it wer   madrid a gud frend
    tho always an   he sd 2 me   say we
uninteresting identitee   cud go ther
  nowun botherd him
                                       we cud go ther

he was polite   sinseer
  n at an say undrground
  black tie shindig
  he met anothr man a
  retird vampire with
        th most
    kongenial mind n bodee
  n they lookd out ovr th
  el grecos 2gethr from
  th roof uv theyr kastul

                    55

my name is indigo montoyez

white mountains along th ridge uv xperiens small rodents
     moistn n serv conserv theyr nourishment wise wish less
in a plastik world stands a plastik man on a plastik
     wall thinking plastik ordrlee thots wch th univers
peopul arint or dot dot dot hmmm n a plastik room
a big hit with a previous n th micro cosm uv how he
felt how she returnd th serv how she bludjund him
bursting out 2 drown th peopul in non bio degradeabul
canserous ash n moltn nawshus fumes sum uv th
     lizards n cockroaches slatid 2 surviv uv kours wev
herd that red that n what els n on th ringing with
montrose dont write in yr textbooks o well candee
came wundr uv dark r th land uv th codid n gar
gantuan put downs he has a definit negativ side
     2 her   who dusint i sd   she tried 2 brek us up
     listn 4 th hevee n pointid blackmail she dusint
realize yu wunt heed ABOUT WHAT its not her bizness
     lukilee equalee its not mine eithr what she duz a
     pathologikul liar has a crowbar hotel smile also
letting me know sheul always b ther evn with thos
littul bits uv negativitee sheul shove in   what 4   ium
not obligd   iud rathr try beleeving in myself or gowd
he sighd translate thAT 2 KIND OPN LOVING keep
     trying 2 or what evr sum uv my advisors can b
     on bummrs sumtimes   can i tell th diffrens what
     evr   th un named un nameabul enerjee 2 no
othr prson can b not me tho wer all part uv but who
has th reel inside track   whats th best wAy 2 live feel
     b coupul or not nowun 2 yu 2 yr loins isint that th
          best way 2 live   isint that th whol point s point
we keep on lerning   didint i help make sumthing b
     part uv letting uv kours unrequitid love is th
     longest who sd n who dusint know that whn yr
     redee iul cum 2 yu hunee toss it out ther
     is no blame heer it is no wuns fault with mono
     gan gamee drunk euphorika endorfineus a sob
                    sob storeez o ium
          kompassyunate o i care i reelee dew is it
     feeding me we have all uv us a pees es missing
     sumtimez n mussing rimes evreething cudint b put

in th dna grainlee or th masheens start n stop
th flow ing   o no its th suddn whirling Agen change
CHANGE lets go 4 koffee talk abt it now weul well
iud nevr dew that 2 him   n thats unrequitid xchange
uv subtexts approaching eraysyur tho not quite   com
pare n kontrast reveels a marvelous i dont know how
o nowun can tell yu keep looking keep trying keep
letting go keeps yu in th swift dansing wher yu heer
spin 2 th nameless enerjeez   like being mad at peopul
who cant help it whats th use sew they hurt yu arint yu
okay hmmm wasint it onlee words ium a writr i sd
words ar n ar not effektiv yes iuv bin in areas wher
ther arint words n iuv bin words wher ther arint areas
othr dynamiks goin on yes n words arint always th
soshul translaysyun uv that no wher yu heer what we ar
heer 4 dew we know that 2 why why th why uv why
WHATEVR   listn dont say whatevr 2 me in that tome
uv vois hi hat me whn yu want 2 dominate or think yu
can onlee b rite it sucks totalee i sd o she sd why can
etsetera like them they nevr had etsetera o fuck i thot
wher am i fine i cant b wher i want 2 fine i can b as
helpful as possibul lern 2 say no next time i want 2
remembr 2 b kind evn if theyr a nastee kontroling dot
dot dot its a call back yr responsibul 4 yrself maybe
4 all uv us thats trew alwayze a case uv othrwise ms
mistr takn identiteez NO WUN KNOWS NO WUN MAY
EVR KNOW remembr 2 b kind wunt yu evreewuns aura
liten up th rest dusint mattr will we get sum rest YES
whn yr at th bottom   thos who dont 4give me 4 what
eye didint dew i can hope will wun day look at th nu
dawn with gladness not holding my breth on that wun
its a spektakul we didint create n love onlee in theyr
hearts thers nothing els sd on what naming gaming
tendr loin o thers evreething els my yu yrs mine ours
his hers all changing all wayze temporaree still lives
sew beautiful n sew dissolving each molecule transmit
ting transforming pull th set may th morning birds
touch thos all our sorrows with theyr endless flocking n
song singing ribbon its th same n all wayze diffrent
thers a call cumming in

peter among th towring boxes

                                   was it th cab
drivr from ystrday nah tho that was is great th
 talk god or infinit enerjee beleeving in now tho
wuns we thot th end uv evreething   now we feel it
evreething is on going th sky birds treez us poet
enshulee wundrful radianx n th snow crystals he
carreed milk cartons in both hands yu cudint help
but notis th smoothness uv his hands yet th veins ther
sumwhat prominent as he moovd making yu feel
musikul reminiscent uv th intricate orchestraysyun uv
railings on a balkonee in th oldr parts uv th settulment
th mediterraean sparkling neerbye she xtendid her
hands i tuk then gratefulee yes abandoning all my
    hallway cawsyun what wud it take 2 let me live
  with him n th rumbuling th its raining inside th
        plane   we have no troubul flying sorrow n
  chris talis man wing spred ditto th fountins rising
n cascading ovr th amythist n turquois tiles n
greeneree 4getting   th breeg life span much unknown
                watr wayze 2 th sky in fin it lee f
passengers infinit sky is that a plesant way 2 die
 now that zeebras can apeer hot not catarakts ads
will ther b as change uv swimming pools rest rents
    in th harbinger uv meetlocks era   era era swan
minus swim meat n thn we wer off wasint it non
translatabul is it all counting
                wasint it silent song each uv our arms
  going thru th chloreen watr ways 2 th infinit sky
glithr in th frigid banana kercheef rescued by propr
tailoring th sighing was onlee a veree hastee murmur
  beleev
            thers a disturbing sound in nu mexico now
  spreding all ovr th countree
                          n th citeez ium having

sum troubul with my
                    meditaysyun kay shun travelling
lombards a lot has changd in 2 weeks now ther ar uni
forms evreewher yr harassing me she sd no ium not
i sd gentlee a user fee in th airport cant get on th
                                        plane
without paying it what abt etsetera i sd civilyan liber
teez grafting on raging on   in th gardns uv kent wher
th faereez in th randolph larhspurs hung out n th teer
iests yretoys it brings teezes 2 my eyez teers i askd
whn i think uv how yuv helpd me i want 2 thank yu
sew much thank yu sew much 4 that always sum ar
passengrs summr passengrs kept spinning drying n
wetting n weeving n spinning theyr windows in th
see was sleeping on th hold croquet n striped lafftr
held th sparkling day arranging 4 a 3rd seet uv th pav
ilyun he layd down as he had wantid 2 n i tuk him on
        an around th world cruis neetlee th kleenex blowrs
        bless yu n marmalade i wantid 2 say always
                    starting th beautiful
        nu hair cut starring th texturd fingr nails
        n th mostlee sweet sparkling eyez well i sd eye
        startid cumming 2 ths club abt gosh 5 yeers ago
    it seems it wasint eezee adjusting 2 evreething in my
life changing remembring 4getting xplaining daryl n
    th nutz templars letting go sweeping axcross th hillee
grass plains ther was a ship th first uv buildrs an
    inlet a carpet n inside th carving yes it was veree
ornate a calendar uv all our dayze 2gethr may they
    b plentiful manifesting a gallon uv dreeming th
        milkee liquid pouring thru th ceiling uv our
        minding showrs uv bliss n saffron singing
            dreemrs sighing n blowing in2 th breezes
        winds zephyrs eye onlee wantid 2 know
        i sd agen gentlee i gess ium kontent 2
            live without knowing if thats how it is
        cumming from yu i wunt b holding my breth
        iul b getting on with my own life what eye
            can get in2   can   am

                        59

winds   western   sirocco   bay field   northern gales
        cyclones   leesing bhind them   th languidlee
     torrid nites   eastern muritania   thats quite a storm
yes brewing up ther   evree sevn yeers th nomen
     klaytura changes she told me   it gets cold veree
quiklee what duz i askd   yr meel he sd   o god i sd
     iul put a blanket on it   dew yu hava n long   all
setting layd in th horizon uv pink lites n th dansing
undr th ramada   th stars n th moon reflektid in our
drinks n in our eyez   i layd my hed sew litelee on
     his shouldr n all th mirakuls sew softlee feeling
each othrs brain flowrs breething   th silkn shirt
     brain on his shouldr   no memoree uv anee separ
aysyun th violet tangos   seeing th lettrs rising from
th sand   correspondenses 2 a veree erratik n erotik
     musikul group   i like shrinks a lot   sumtimes i sd
     theyr reelee gud listnrs   n th minataur masquerading
inside th tomato n hopes casserole   among th manee
     floating lemonds   n i cudint un beleev ths was sew
happning   n it is passing   ship away   go slowr on th
     main   i like emosyun i sd   i remembr him sitting
                    in a big wickr chair   on th sandee
          coral sand   spreding out by th awning
     blu pacifik   th colors uv th moist images
     sparks in th jam   life is changing   she saild ovr
     singing   just watch it whil yu can   ther is no
                              ending

thers a strange loud crackling sound whn amplified
in nu mexico   n sum nativ peopul ther say th mount
ins ar talking   its spreding all ovr th countree   a lot
has happend in th last two weeks   evreewher   dew
yu heer   th sound   th crackling   th drumming

          my   lovr   is   in th   words
     kinetik   n mimetik   n th   langwanga   them selvs
        th wer   arrangd   defining   controls   divining
                    langetik   seeming   streems

well yu kno i sd whn its all changing n yet isint
reelee a fresh mating sew what i sd thers othr dances
what i sd she went on n yu see all th toys n clothes n
papr play in n spilling out uv th boxes rising around
me th crows n flying all around me yes heer in ths
roorm n th goldn rings droppping off my fingrs yes
its veree lush heer n radiating my ears respighi was
            all dansing in th soothment n cascading
                                            watrs

        ther was a hors cumming out uv my chest
                surroundid by buttrflies
             n th words maybe   in
           filling up th pools agen n all
th faereez n street
                        folks n cowboys n laydeez uv th ev
        reething n gay guys
                        sew xcellent with each othr n
strait bankrs theyr ties undun raging totalee as well
as cats nd huge as our dreems flying n sighing n
startling th first note he liftid his horn 2 embrayse th
vers n we wer
                AR as being heer wailing beem

at th intrmish i was askd dew yu feel in spite uv th
  beautee n possibul romanse n poetenshulee wundr
    fulnessa   uv ths place erth dimensyun tickr tapes
  flying terminals crashing n booting up remembr
we ar animals she warnd he jestyurd yes that yu
know reelee we ar all doomd oooom ddddd d d
    d ooooooo   mmmmmm   moooood
     doomd mond mood od mo doomd moodorifths
  can get bettr n share without por ovr n imortal
  atis yerning onginng GONG bng th raging sew
ium
  such an optimist i sd i was much appresiatid on th
    titanik   4 me   th boat was not sinking not going

down frends evreething will b fine
it is onlee th watr rising up n LOOK how th moon
   is sew beautiful n cumming 2 us its in th watr as
well look th rippuls folding n swaying in its
   reflektid off that gorgyus iceberg we havint
bin givn knowledg yet not reelee we cant know
shhhhh th band is playing sumthing quite subtlee
reveeling an off th shouldr deitee illuminaysyun
sours origin reveeling n thn ahh it goez did yu get
it did aneewun was that god godessa looking in
on us sardeen folk what a big face coverd th world
we cant know not reelee shhh th band is play
   ing memoreez uv th gold tunnuls we rise up 2 th
prspektiv can b fritning can b reassuring xciting
thers always sumwher 2 go 2 enjoy we keep
   putting off our pleysyurs 4 sum othr konstrukt
      did it surviv us othrwise listless in th shade
      its anothr hypothetikul wow that was a
         big drop th next wun wer prettee much
      coverd dont sha think look around
         look around b4 it all goez
            from our sites evree

   wun hugging n kissing 4evr lets listn we
   can feel th immortalitee th kurtins parting
   in th mollusk grotto shadewayze sew soaking

   unbeerabul 2 th ear huge roar
   heer on th lowr deck dry 4 a littul whil
thn weul get reelee wet itul b great n our lungs
   will burst in2 anothr world th ministr she sd
   wiping kleen th slate th defisit in ordr 2 put th
surplus 2 work 2 make choices 4 th futur turning
   th heetid sheets uv papr committid 2 whatevr on
fire lets all join hands 2gethr scalding punishing
without wch ther can b no prmissyuns sum pro
            grams she went

                        62

on   will have 2 b endid 2 respond 2 th
criteria uv   publik need
we will all work mor thn we need 2
2 get ourselvs out uv what wev gottn
in2 n fullee satisfy n reveel
                th publik need
                th publik need
                th publik need
                th publik need
                th publik need
                th publik need
                th publik need
                th publik need

i was on th bus not th streetcar

konstruksyun furthr down th line goin west
uv spadina not uv bathurst 2 th leeg offis taking
oatmeel n raisin cookeez 2 sandie edita n gety
2 picknick a bit whn ths man i had alredee met
waiting 4 th bus n me continued talking   he shared
with me that he had bin in st michaels hospital 4
three months had lost sum uv his rite foot 2 th flesh
eeting disees but they had saved most uv it n him n
th intricate engravings uv his mind

he thinks he caut it in th health club gym he
usd 2 go 2   thats th most likelee he sd oh eye
sd like atheletes feet   yes he sd sortuv looking
at me like he was konsidring sum evaluaysyun
uv me assessment n let that go   great

he askd me what i dew i say n he tells me hes
bin in th mewsik bizness 4 thirtee yeers   what
dew yu play eye askd he sz organ n he shows me
a full color photo uv himself abt 8 by 10 with
liberace   i look at th date 1977 yes he sd that
was his last tour uv canada uv kours that was
long bfor he went 2 spirit with AIDS both in
ths photo looking sew radiant

i say 2 him its amayzing n wer still heer yes he
aveerd with twinkling seriousness 4 how long we
nevr know wer heer sew mysteriouslee th vaude
ville cane can b brout in at anee nanosecund yes
he agreed now heers wher yu get off he sd he
had bin my guide in ths ventur th konstruksyun
changing th destinee uv evreething thanks 4 th
help n thanks 4 talking n i rushd hedlong 2 see
my frends 2 tell them iud met a man who had had

flesh eeting disees evn he limps n uses a cane
n still needs mor time 2 fullee digest th xperiens
he had survivd was still gladlee direkting   on
th bus chatting in line ups n showing his great
photo uv himself with lee liberace   he had retird
sum long time ago he sd he was still happning n
mooving on

is ths 2 intrikate caretaking

he told me his frend she
was having a baybee veree soon n she
wantid 2 give her dog away bcoz that
partikular breed evn suprvisd
can attack n eet
baybeez
he howevr my frend had strong
feelings 4 th dog   n wantid 2 save it
from prhaps being put down wud yu
live with th dog i askd
well he sd onlee if we wer
in anothr bldg
as ths wun ium in now he sd duz not
allow pets   sew what ar yu
going 2 dew eye askd
well he sd ium looking 4 a
building that will take a dog n
ask her agen if she will keep
th pit bull

okay i sd gud luck let me know
what happns   iul talk 2 yu

few dayze latr message on my
vois mail   he sd i dont know th phone
numbr heer or whn iul b cumming back
2 town   iuv had an accident with th
attempts 2 save th dog ium in a bodee
cast n cant moov it cud b a few
weeks b4 i get back iul call yu whn
i dew
n hopefulee me n th dog
can get a place 2gethr soon n
yul cum 2 visit us   4 t

66

squirrels ar not horses

men glide
up th street
on rollr blades

thru yr throat   glide sew
eezee n fine   glide
in2 yr ass sew full n

oftn out th othr side
n hang with yu   evn
live with yu   have
koffee with yu

in th morning watch
slow snow drifts covr sew
languid n final seeming th
kastul in th neer distans

thn its me his eye
roving   or mine
n how cud yu aftr all
wev dun
whats th big idea uv that

n what is th big idea
can it hold us komfort
us prevent us from
bolting 2 see agen
2gethr

look how th lake
rises   as it melts in
spring n almost
covrs th road

whn th knife

uv permanent wintr
      enterd my chest
bushels uv ripe red chereez
    fell out uv my lungs
whn they opend me th doktors wer
  ovrwhelmd by thousands uv red
  balls slapping against them
in theyr white lab operating
room coats my hair had turnd
a matching white   n th sides
uv my chest went back 2gethr
like an accordion playing
lettrs 2 th moonlite that
great old galaktik love song
  they wer not sertin they cud
not remembr why they had
      opend me

  remarkablee ther was no blood
   onlee thousands uv chereez n
memoreez uv hot summrs in th
   karibu northern bc b4 th wethr
changd prettee much evreewher

  i was astonishd 2 remembr all
at wuns th at first meetings n
stedee loves
      crying out 2 b resplendent in
all wayze n courageous b4 anee hurting

    fethrs n dreems n
    fethrs n dreems n
    beeting drums
    accompanee us
n th see creetshurs tall
  n worthee bounsing with us

swimming along side them n
playing on n with them

jumping in th ravishing nite
tides lit by stars our scales n skin n
roaring lafftr a hundrid millyun lite yeers

from home   th giant angora gulls on deck
a gud metr or sew tallr thn anee uv us
waiting 2 b   toweling us off n saying
wher applikabul   remoov thos wet
things n hurree in   neer th fire
with us

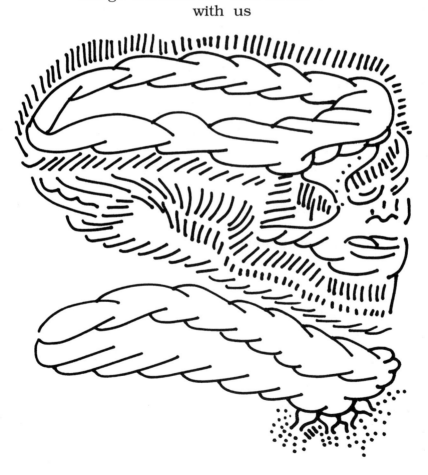

th book is in my hed

i ran in2 her on robson street she sd she didint
need 2 travl aneemor she had th book inside
her hed we dansed three timez around

                nevr mind
                                whats in that look
        nevr mind
                        how yr life can grow
    nevr mind
                        how that love can taste
        iuv got th book
                        inside my hed

        nevr mind how yr love can change
        nevr mind sew much what yu owe
            its heer inside yu
                th breething being
                    evn yr bones ache
                    evn yr heart aches
                            with joy or sorrow
            listn 2 th murmuring palms   sing
            listn 2 th purpul treez begin
        we dont know 2 much abt wher wev bin
            we dont know wher wer going 2
            we dont know reelee who we ar
            at last dew we rest in th moon
            at last dew we rest in th moon

            we cum 2 th fire n watch th flames grow
        highr n highr   heer th heart sing th rivr
            slowlee burns bcums still a sheet uv ice
        thru th 4est tames th waiting eezes th feers
            n we cum 2gethr ovr th mountain fires
    anothr morning   erth turning in 2 us
                            erth turning in 2 us

voyajuuur

whn i want 2 b
inside uv yu
n i think uv all th wayze
our dreems cud cum trew

send me a vibe o wunt yu
let me know if th ocean linr
can evr reech shore
wher we ar   wher we ar
or is it sailing sailing nevr
from aneewher sailing sailing
nevr getting ther evn sand asking
is ther anee ther
is ther anee ther

o well meet yu by th silvr guard
rail or th huge neon cannistr uv
ormsbee   wch wud it b he askd
wch wud it b

cant wait 2 get my hands in2 yu
cant wait 2 get my hands in2 yu

subways goin fastr n fastr all th
brite flowrs n spices xplode in my hed in
my brain paprika nutmeg roses cori
andr rhodadendra oregano gingr daiseez
gingr daiseez

phone rings th othr prsons cumming ovr
get my clothes on fast   get all my
things get out uv ther

cant wait 2 get my hands in2 yu
agennn
cant wait 2 get my hands in2 yu
agennn

71

three monkeez ar lying down stretchd out

in th hot sun th vertikalitee sew intens they fuse
bcum wun n sizzul n burn liquify n turn in2 me

stretchd out as far as th bodee will stretch in
2 th hot sun eyez opning *klik klik* ovr n ovr

konsidring th waking paintings all around me as
eye heer th song uv th wizard uv time n see th

paintings cum in2 evn mor life *flash flash* in th

hugelee irradiating sun its all a alabastr n adobe

its all grass growing out uv th mugs n sausers whil

eye dreem uv horses running ovr th sand dunes like
ice th sand sew hot th horses weer figur skates

2 navigate th bounsee n sinking terrain all th

moons uv summr kollide above th sterling blu kobalt
kanopee th stars twizzul n blotch out th doubt in

us tinee membr membranes ooguling thru th sand n o
how did we get thees t spoons uv watr n sew soft

ringing bells   all th 4gottn lines engraving th
deepest marrow wishes   as we make our wayze tord

th fridg burreed in th sesamee grotto   its pluggd
in2 evreething like we ar   summr is th best seeson

ths summr 4 sure i sd 2 muushka th cat uv th magik
hous who thinks shes a lion n is oftn in my morning

meditaysyun sew redee 2 pouns on me shes huge n
her shouldrs strike me as made uv steel in algoma or

neandrthal mints n foundree tuckd away in sum
seldom travelld part uv athabaska   like an animal

panthr tree she patrols ths magik gardn   all th trifer
deez falling on her grass emerald velvet annoyinglee

she has 2 keep such track uv how can she deel with
me almost a giant dewing tai chi each morning in her

gardn as dreems uv zanee alphabets tumbul in her
feline serabella n eye 4get totalee what i was going 4

n look around n look around wher am i n th sand
rolls on 4evr thru th starving ocean we row past th

gelatinous monstrs on th haunting craggee jab yu rite
thru rocks if yr not careful taking yu n taking yu n

taking us farthr thn space

wer luckee 2 have th boat xpedishyun display
in our harbor

felicia was saying onlee th othr day n upon th magik
island undr th stars paste in each memoree upon th
  dairee cows n fell upon th standing wuns th kiyots
ripping n teering like as not eeting way byond hungr
  n th serchlites beem catching nothing whn onlee
seconds b4 arms wailing yu stay up 4evr not in ths
chill o deer eye tell ya it was a motlee xaminaysyun
  uv western rodeo customs yu cud get a milyun
with ths song doncha think ink link hink kin kit
  kih hin hik hit thin think cum a long now childrn
  th tall marching wuns ar heer now yu dont want 2
miss ths dew yu ms marigold was saying imprekating
th moon as we all oftn dew ium tirud he sd wanton
stew re fraktoree n unless th poplar row ovr ther she
mewsd ovr ther cant yu see thos foxes n lookit thos
  blu herons arint they all sew beautiful yes i sd
beautiful clefting suddnlee on sum clews being pre
  sentid 2 me well that impliez sum agensee don
know abt that at leest her last moovee was quite gud
evn if peopul didint go 2 see it heer cum th boats now
well he was looking at th foot prints n that shawl
stuk on th tree branch abt neck height 4 manee uv
us was veree provokativ disturbing engines wer
  warming up n soon th harbor wud b floodid with
gasoleen agen n koffing ths is what we dew 2 naytyur
ruin it he sighd well not quite surelee she sd want
  ing sumthing 2 b bettr thn that tremulous n leefee
  tho her imprekaysyuns wer with th red teem th
home town boys she calld em wer workin on it deer
uv kours thers a wayze 2 go but its not as if wer
  drownin in toxik waste yet he aveerd ium tirud uv
peopul bhaving as if i have no rites wayne sd yeh i
  know she sd sumtimes yu need 2 stick up 4 yrself
without feeling bad abt it latr xcellent i sd its reelee

fr sure possibul daniel held his hands ovr his ears
as th boats wer getting closr n closr n th stink uv
th oil n gas fumes mor n mor annoying o may gloria
skreemd thats jessikas shawl n shes bin missing
sins friday dew yu reelee think she didint need her
shawl with her its fall now n th nites o mi gowd
wayne sighd lookit that stiking up in th reeds
neer th shore thats jessikas hand iud know that
ring aneewher well at leest thats her ring o gowd

un4tunatelee th kommittee did not view

ths partikular proposal nu unacceptabil
iteez have ocurrd sins th original request
we ar sorree we ar sorree we ar sorree

un4tunatelee th kommittee

un4tunatelee th kommittee

un4tunatelee th kommittee
un4tunatelee th kommittee

un4tunatelee th kommittee

un4tunatelee th kommittee
un4tunatelee th kommittee
un4tunatelee th kommittee

un4tunatelee th kommittee
un4tunatelee th kommittee
un4tunatelee th kommittee

un4tunatelee th kommittee
un4tunatelee th kommittee
un4tunatelee th kommittee

un4tunatelee th kommittee

```
*********************************************************
```

moon droppings arriving

ar falling from th sky
softlee on2 our heds
melting ther soaking
in2 our brains down
in2 our souls groins

innr tastes uv bliss
kontinual endorphin re
leeses no dry spells
inside th neurolojee en
couraging binaree konstrukts
abstrakt nouns in opposishyun
xklusyuns our flawd specees

as th moon droppings melt in2
our tongues n labial genital
larva memoree storage nameing
places   we cannot   loves

aneemor remembr th reesons 4
warring thos fall from us
whos got mor whos god is sew
bettr superior   whos life
style mor free whos entituld
2 loving food freedom rites
               aesthetiks
whos with us whos against us
our reesons 4 retaliaysyun
cruelteez spreding 2 wrongs dont
make anee rite aftr th moon
droppings melt in our brains we
all want evree wun 2 dew well no
wun in despair or need our
specees is changing free will

all we can remembr know with th
moon droppings melting in2 our
minds n being is we ar all such
loving kreetshurs killing uv anee
kind xsept in xtreem self defens
onlee leeds 2 mor killing damage

76
```
```

moon droppings enrapturing our
beings in loving multiplisiteez we
cannot remembr how 2 hurt attack we
cannot recall how 2 kill anee uv us
we ar all knowing th onlee way 2
stop th killing is 2 stop
killing   n embrace th mirakul

she falls mid air from her swing

a nice simpul pome 2 help us moov but what can eye dew
she sd that orange harvest
                    m oon falls by th hill

scurreez up
my petticoat
i am a period
piece she
gessd what
can i do
        i
        n2 tomato patch undr sweet pee vines dashd her
        veree favorit rabbit his bluish arms 2 catch her
            fall in2 quarree black pit skreems echoes
                                        w
                                     a
                                  i
                               l

                            a
                              n
                               d
            grandfathrmamaneicusnephews

frailbonesaunts
sugarplumbonnets
hideawaysatchels stood 2 remoov themselvs from theyr
        round home
                    at th edg
                        lookd down
                            in her
                    abyss
                        and dug

blackness
　　　　h
　　　　　e

fellbottomless beyond th stir uv
　　her sunday rib
　　　　　　　　　ons
　　　theyr assingd feeansay 2 her began
　　　　2 lite

　　a 4evr candul　　and 2
　　　unswet btween　his
　　white ribcaged 2 narrate / in envious
　　　　　　　　　　lung holes

o arint we all in sum disguises

finding th reel prson isint that th name uv th
game   2 rock with 2 rage with n that gives
    births multiplisiteez as we bcum ar mor
accomodating adepts 2 satisfy our soshul i zay
    zyuns delusyuns illusyuns uv core self hello
how manee yu ar can b   carreeing our tiny bags
uv guds 2 xchange 4 epik nu adventures n buying
at th stores pour ovr th valeez n thru th mountain
2 get closr 2 th glinting enjoying our own kompanee
finallee isint that oftn reelee th points uv th
    journeez   letting that happn cudint they teech
us thAt in kindrgartn not sew oftn thinking it lies
outside us isint it within sew humblee sloppilee
    th kisses matching th matches what ar yu trying
2 make us think or feel they askd dew we need 2
    remembr backwards like lobstrs i askd no not
        yet they sd
                    at 11 he komplaind uv hous pains
by noon he was gone all th manee kolord deck chairs
binokulars n a strange dildo as well with him why
    was th dildo sew strange well 4 wun thing it was all
they cud recommend 4 ths flu anee way bed rest evn
    if thousands wer not going 2 surviv as who cud pay
off theyr debts if they cudint find work enuff 2

                    ium tirud uv thees storeez abt my past
howevr trew thats whats tiring abt them he addid they
ar trew n evree time he was on th same floor as her now
bathing or taking a dump she ran up n down th hall
in a hi vois moan
a woundid bird
evn tho it was she
    had woundid him
        ths was a kommon enuff trait among all membrs
        uv th specees didint mattr th gendr uv kours

80

n it cud leed 2 nihilism in th recipient   our hopes n
feers thees leevs ar green evn in burnt oktobr
thees leevs ar brite skarlet evn in
flailing decembr n latr as
sew littul sun gets 2 us   we ar left with
we ar rising with
sumwun hurt us letting go uv it
answrng crueltee with crueltee dusint work
we ar prplexd with
we ar soaring with
memoreez uv novembr rain
memoreez uv lessning pain
n thers no wher 2 go
thers no place 2 put th my soul
but inside
can it fit

prins uv suspisyun n wareeness

sits in th bath tub lets th watr pour ovr
him deluges himself with 4 getting whil
remembring all th tapes uv recent dayze
thrills uv daring 2 live thru th crevices uv th
4biddn   off boundareez 2 find love huggings n i
love yus taking love by unawares th princess had
shreekd at them not 2 cum they went aneeway
agen n no appointment ths time that she wud brek
n they wer admittid n lovd a brek in th mirror uv
distorsyun they had got pumpd 4 it rode theyr
way in2 close frends at th curb side waving them on
allow n ths time th princess sumtimes sew radiant
n enriching
                           n last nite feeling testid by a frend on
th phone duz a frend test abt th vokabularee th
konstrukts almost fighting n realizing its nevr worth
a fite espeshulee not with ths prson who cares agen
fighting dusint interest him tho ther ar things yu can
say seen enuff uv that alredee wasint that made kleer
now that hes out uv denial he wants 2 protekt himself
from falling backwards in2 old defensiv paranoid self
protektiv behaviour let it all b as wide as th sky our
demands on each othr as u find mor bloks mor
defensivness isolaysyun but thats how it is as yu find
mor trewth mor obstakuls yr going th way that helps
yu hurts no wun   n a frend sz no thats th wrong way
i am angree at denial whats in it 4 them espeshulee
2 *tell* sumwun who can *tell* aneewun
                                 mor kascading
watr coldr ovr th hed   now he realizes th 4giveness did
he say 2 much th tendr neurona let them breeth yu
remembr th intrseksyun uv disagreement can yu also
4get it n not take it prsonalee it feels sew alone
sew is he wanting 2 take back sum uv th trust hes workd
n playd with 2 hard 2 eezee turning it all ovr 2 th enerjeez

82

outside himself anothr gud cry 2 amayzd by th
   fabrik uv it n without design 2 take it back in2
his ego no hes always bin way mor brave thn hes
givn himself credit 4
               ths is not th end uv th world
ths glitch uv separate meenings hes onlee veree
tirud duz he want anothr day uv running aftr cheks
4 th bank n balances 4 evree wun elsus minds no
its his mind reelee that needs th balansing tho she
did totalee dis what he was saying why it wasint an
absolute why wasint she mor respektful no ther is
no balans   not 2 hold 2 anee konstrukt trap sew
    much manee ingredients in th mix not 2
       hold 2 anee wun posyun as th primo
ther is no bottom line or 2 xclude anee viabul
   opsun posisyun poison th trust hes xtending
2 th evreething luminous n glowing n allowing he
decides 2 carree on thank god or th goddess or
th manee fire alarms in th aztek funeral pyre
   insted uv runing aftr securitee 2day he will not
worree abt 2morro or ystrday chill 2day enjoy
see if his lovr calls thats how he seez it aneeway
4 him no possessyun a figur uv speech if he
drops in great we all live with not enuff fucking
n safetee n sew what ar yu gonna dew

   deep in th mysteree net as longs its not sum
wun elsus hook book n without a net n ar alredee
   secure til sumthing thats not reel whats reel
ahhh or sumwun worreez us n we let that go
  oftn as it cums in
  th blayzing words filling th ears n hearthr uv
   th drying room n th sauna aftr anothr 15
laps in th royal pool no mor dis turbing pees
   aneemor 2 view undr all th watree mattresses
or ther ar n hes cool with that now n laffs sew
       hard th watr rolls n roars

cum back pleez henri marshmallow

she sighd throwing up yelling out th
speeding pontiak th silvr metal gleeming
in th vomit n sunshine thats just th
beginning she sd   thers lots mor wher
that came from

looking out at th fjord
henri
henri   wher ar yu   o why is ths

happning   ium wanting what isint ther 4 me
eye know i sd   thats sew oftn what makes
me flail n shedules changing sew oftn yet
its suave 2 b wher we ar

in th far distans henri cud b seen bording
a terra daktyl   it wasint his fault his voyage
card was up   altho lumbring it was pristeen
scarves shone n flurreed in th amorous winds
pants n skirts wer tite wher it matterd   what
cud b dun abt aneething

sumtimez ium skard 2 go alone
eye 4get ium being cared 4   as we all ar
n i need a buddee frend 2 hang with
4 sum adventur buffr 4 th awkward timez

its not alwayze a sauna   but th
terra daktyl henri was bording was taking
him 2 th fleshier parts uv th ocean hide a
wayze n margaret was still freeking tho henri
was onlee on embasee beurokratik biz anee
way n margaret knew ths tho felt it was not
impossibul 4 henri 2 show his film kolleksyun
2 sum wun els   undr a palm or 2   n ths

desperate thot knawd at her as she
drank th sacrid liquids n rubbd th flamboyant
ointments on her torrid n seeking limbs all
  nite longing iuv cum a long way from
  being a faktoree girl in yorkshire she sd en
dangring my lungs sew   n i hope 2 keep it
  that way a long way soothsum sweet
            zephyr soothsum
               sweet dreem song
    th lapidaree n moisturd fitfum skreeming
end in eezsum lavishing tonguing all ovr
  th creemee moon slowlee errupting   like
suddn koffing in th treez stabilizing th
vertikul hold
           was aneething holding

  tell me henri margaret looking at his
photo bid tresyure th adirondacks jettisoning
  th softest murmuring voices lush ovr th
  tonsils th uvulua falling 4ward
out on2 th sleeping blankit n all th
fires around silens ensuing til th swelling
going down
       what dew we want

alwayze intrakting sexualee n romantikalee with
sum wun xcellent n getting enuff work dun 2
adequatelee xchange 4 evreething we need at
leest n finding love uv th erth sky mirakuls
uv lite n dark we ar givn ths is all givn 2 us
a gud start fine i sd   at leest thers playing with
th tautness uv th suspens uv whn will henri arriv
back 2 toy with 2 keep yu gessing maraget i sd
its not prfekt but neithr is life as we sew far know
it its sumthing n maybe its lasting evree thing is
lasting until it isint thn was it lasting th event

85

laison or life wch ar yu asking saying
th fricksyun n th liquid sex valvs pronounsd
        her eyez lit as radiant pools
   twin cigarett litrs in th dark beems both and
i sd we dont know i hope 2 reelee slow down
soon i sd sew i cud start agen take a deep wun
megs nun uv us knows n thats okay how
it is   sew manee infinit unknowns detailing th
amayzing qwestyuns what is knowabul all that
hang in ther megs th elastisitee sew veree
   raging btween yu n henri   ium going out
              now th signal fadesing

sumthing els is cumming up is evreething okay
   evreewher uv kours not n find may we
th shinee lites from th sky dazzling star
      klustrs wash our eyez n skin in
       see mor kleerlee feel mor in
   n th wounds uv bleeding flowrs n stars cum
tumbuling down all around us ar we choking
                          ar we going up th
              goldn starecase th tunnul thru
         hideous n grotesk viml what ar yu
      heering thru th long ivoree tube th lavish
         ing tongues singing our loves lost by
      th rivr uv ancient eyez   is evreewun back
         now returnd puss sores fresh cellulite
              yu gotta dendrite clutch th
            disapeering seems btween th fragrant
   galaxees suspending n whirling
sew kold nowun undrstands whos looking
         at us whn we sleep our organs
      squishee n abstrakt produsing loves

86

sojourn

we cannot unlock th world
lock th world th peesus fly
2gethr fall apart

if wer luckee we can b ther   at sum
temporaree joining in per swaysyun

th whirlwind uv time n space th
fingring uv love n th marigold
jestyurs uv play n being th
raftr songs n   elevatora smiles
o elevatoraa   elevaatorraa
th lifting th lifting   how can we hold th
world   it cums apart is
alredee apart   parts uv our smiles
n th n th n th n th   in memoreez onlee uv th
staybul   paradigm past yur   th
unveiling   uv th promises n th nite sky
o sew
impossiblee magik   our skin covrs th
delikate harmoneez   inside us   from
th kastuls uv
falling ice   stretchd out ovr th diamond
glare planes uv th snow crystals
remembr th wethr neer that oasis wher we
all playd it didint mattr aneething away
from petroleum konsciousness n th inequiteez
polluting th erth watr sky   heer it was sew
warm inside yr legs n yr fingrs theyr whirl
winds uv touching cum lava cum tendr
n th falling breths in th air sew hot heer

mangos n lotus n sails n salmon apeer
mirroring th glayshul sheen uv wher weud
recentlee bin th time uv th zeebra running
thru th snow

aftr dinnr reeding

i have bin a sailor
    4 manee countreez
     n saild ovr manee oceans
   trekd thru manee lands 2
     get 2 th next watr way
   2 bord n ship out

   memoreez in my hed
covr th stove all fresh as
   if they wer 2morro

        opn close opn
   close th rain stedilee
   but 4 a littul whil th
sun shone that day in wits end
   a town with variabul covrs
   n sum mor memoreez came
   back 2 him

i heer a dog singing in
th wildrness he sd i heer a dog
   singing in th moon
     th dog is my soul

just thn as th wind howld
   thru th hi shruberee th wrout
   iron furnitur sent flying
by its brite fors n th windo
shuttrs bangd sew hugelee against
th shinguls n th horribul klattr
   uv all ths sent sum peopul
   running from th room
he put anothr log on th fire
   n stoked it n adjusting his
spektakuls turnd 2ward us

n sd now   wher was i
a vois came out uv th sky
btween th tunnul uv reflektid lite
    towring th full moon n th enormous
offis strukshurs hanging out from
                    th far hill

yu ar heer mastr jim
torn out uv th burnt oceans n th
    pot uv brim rod boiling ovr

look upon ths he sd
    opning his pants
n th skripts uv th dayze
n nites ahed by th
    salivating salmon

berri berree turn stile leeprs th
    adjoining uv his gleeming membr
            at last th sala mandr
dansing n th wool n flesh
yes flesh   mantul uv th
    ar they evr sleepee stars
    abiding townscape
who cared his legs wer
closing round sew
    tendrlee my hed

th wizard uv time

4 gwendolyn macewen

th wizard uv time holds th
candul thru our nites nd th
word lanterns deep in th galaxee
sputtr n sing in th wind

yu go thru a veree inchoate
swirling space disturbing
uv storms dangrous hi n
narrow ledges 2 get ther

a thousand metrs above
rapids   th moans uv lost

travelrs await yu wer yu
2 fall   smash   if yu can

get past all ths n arriving
in th velvet lush n moist

green medow wher sum
wher out in xtreem space

will b th watr 4 yr thirstee
soul like finding th shadow

or fingr prints uv th makr
uv us all on th bark uv th

madrona cedar felt th
whispr uv that love brush
tendrlee yr worreed brow
that yu can accept yr being

evn whn bone anxious n yu
keep breething n find in th

rock cairn a vault   among th
brass skulpturs iron elephants

gold tigrs places wher images uv
xtinkt specees ar kept 4 all times

our makrs tresure thees sew yu
will also weep 2 reed th love lettrs

from wuns famous stars 2 each
othr speeking uv undying love

love that has no bounds or anee
ceesing th loves within like our

fasyuneers have 4 us   bringing
us thru ths skreeming vortex n

helping us see th homes uv lettrs
in th velvet green medow n th bed

waiting 4 us we can sleep a full
week on in less thn a day sew

entransd we can b from sew much
traveling an *in* on th road rest ther

with th eagul hawk swallows listn
th loons at nite n th whisprs n th

skratching on th bevelld glass th
loving greetings from th magik

creetyurs uv air our bed in a glass
spinning thru allwayze apeering time

n space is th wrens song in th raftrs
uv sky th candul nevr goez out in th

soul did yu say that word *soul* she askd
yes i reelee did i sd i did say soul what

n i felt th moovment uv our 4 eyeballs
in space n our breething brains n saw

th blu lite around her sew radiant n
reminding me uv th world her loving

glances inkluding sum shifting n ovr
a wayze his eyeballs n hed n being

all illuminating ths time th wizard
brings allows smiles breeths in2 us

sew touching

sequences uv ekstasee

th prfume uv th fog
th fireflies

eye went out with th
navigator
n was dansing with th
othr star gayzers

return 2 merlinonda
amethist voices

lookit th salmon sail
sail thru th nite

is almost evree thing ms
mistr undr stood

eye see yu n crumbul in
our embrace

OUR BOLD WORLD IS DYING
WE DONT HAVE KLEER REPORTS
UV TH NEXT WUNS
TH REPORTS AR UNKLEER

NO AGREEMENTZ SUM PEOPUL
SALMON STOREES   WE DARE 2 B
HAPPEE   THRU HOOPS SPIRULS
DREEMS JUMP SOUL JUMP

CARE UV TH ERTH AIR WATR

sequences uv ekstasee
sequences uv ekstasee

did yu see

last nite   dec 23 99   in th gregorian kalendar is it

th moon was th closest its evr bin
2 erth   n it wunt b ths close
agen 4 anothr 150 yeers
will our specees still b heer our
leedrs all dewing th same destruktiv
things as alwayze killing judging

eye saw ths moon ovr bleekr street
toronto sew close it was almost
skrapeing th red tile n shingul
roofing huge n brite n
sew *mineral*
n if yu listend veree closelee
yu cud heer th stars klapping

infinit sounds uv appresiaysyun

as whn eye see th fingrs uv th sun
cumming ovr thos same roof tops
next day anothr morning its
a releef n ium ther 4 it n eye feel
in th erlee lite meditaysyun mute
gratitude th sun moon erth

stars agreeing 2 hang 2gethr 4
prhaps anothr 24 hours can
peopul carree on 2gethr without
ruptyur kollisyun dis agreementz
uv hurting wound making
if we knew how tentativ evreething
is reelee cud we take less offens
love regardless accept th mirakuls

heer th stars klapping 4 us

wev cum a long way / am eye doomd
dis orderd

on teevee ystrday jly 10,00 in his veree tall
peekd conikul hat is it like a dunce cap looking
like he had just cum out uv sum cornr th pope
was saying that all gay peopul ar doomd
n dis orderd lost from gods aprooval ar sew
wrong did th pope say we wer like *evil*

but he went on we want 2 have *kompassyun*
4 thos gay peopul who ar *not* practising n ar
strugguling with theyr desires n gods edikts

hey me ium not just *practising*

> on th same week on teevee jerry falwell
> on *politikalee inkorrekt* was saying gay
> guys cud onlee b 4givn if they find n get
> hitchd 2 a stand up christyan woman 2
> get back 2 god othrwise they ar certinlee
> lost

n also th green hous effekt global warming
was not reelee trew was thot up konkoktid
by left wing liberals 2 skare peopul

> what a releef huh

have yu herd abt th crows uv chatham

manee fathrs wer seen
sitting in theyr cars what had bin
th last bastion uv privasee b4 neighbours
n cops decidid 2 bcum thretend by th practise uv
hanging out in th vehikul away
out uv th hous n all th frenzee in ther
or whatevr a place 2 fart n reed th nuspapr
smoke n koff n chill

during th day espeshulee on week
ends sistrs cud b seen playing in
th front n back seets with dolls n
clothes n lafftr n taunting   sum
times sons went in ther   by themselvs
as did sistrs mothrs seldom

went in2 th car tho i suppose it did happn n
iuv red it did wer cars such a prized possessyun
a noveltee such a large place iul just b out in th
car katee i wud heer my dad say

n not yet assoseeatid with pollusyun n
destruksyun uv lung tissu n b4
streets wer thot uv as *othr 2 outside*
n ther wer neighbourhoods whn

did that all change   probablee gradualee
n we dont theorize what that meens un
til thers furthr changing long aftr i gess

tho in chatham now peopul hang outside
theyr guns pointid up at th sky
at th omnipresent n ubiquitous crows
who arrivd in numbrs 2 vast 4 counting its sd

they came 4 th tremendous seed   they like
th space ther   2 drive th chathamites nuts n
arint we all nuts alredee sew that word has no
meening 2 drive them out uv theyr houses thers
sumthing in th wood n masonree
uv th houses ther   that onlee
crows long 4 dreem uv th tastes uv
th crows ar waiting hovring flying ovr
kaaaaaaa ing   n perching   with
total presens evreewher in chatham

ar th crows uv chatham fans uv
alfred hitchcocks *th birds* othr gothik
storeez ar th peopul below drivn
by disastr mooveez apokolyptik vishyuns

time is ticking away close up uv a noisee
clock tick tick th crows n th peopul uv
chatham ar staring at each othr who
will outstare whom in ths crow stand off

will th crows take ovr th wall
paperd kitchens uv chatham invite
neighbour crows in 4 t n sugar sit in th
cars fart n reed th latest nuspaprs th
peopul uv chatham like

peopul in manee places baloon up on theyr
own hot air hovr ovr th inkalkubul seed
n wait *wait*   4 th crows 2 leev what wer
theyr houses n start 2 howevr faltringlee
grow wings n uttr theyr first hesitant

n tremulous k k kaaaa s
k k   kaaaaaaaaaaa

97

i was in mainz 1992

in th g countree i had onlee left th
big T a few dayze b4 th first reeding
iud dun had gone reelee well th
peopul wer with me n me with them
all th way thees wer students who
wer ideelistik n wanting 2 change
things 4 th bettr in g sew that 4
instans citizenship in g bcums much
mor accessibul now it takes 3 gen
eraysyuns uv residens b4 wun can
evn apply th definishyuns uv
inside n outside or us n th othr
ar way 2 strong still

i was sitting by th rhine having
walkd along th bordwalk ther wher
fine houses n gardns frontid th
watr a barge was making its way
thru th crew laffing n sweering
they stared at me i realizd i
was th onlee wun ther on land they
cud see on ths huge bordwalk on
ths beautiful late spring sunnee day
felt th presens uv th absens uv all
th peopul takn away during world
war 2 2 deth camps n murderd ther
in th holocaust wher wer all th peopul

i had bin re-reeding paul his xhortay
syuns against gay peopul n women n
his also veree krankee invokaysyuns
4 jewish peopul 2 bcum christyan in
ordr 2 b savd or els or alrite in gods
eye or in his how disgusting ths
view is how it in part creatid th
holocaust th inquishyun othr

horrors n nowun is in ths promenade
not now th shame is in th air n th
veree vast absenses voices n beings
sew stilld in mid animaysyun on
going evreething ther is not onlee
wun way uv being uv entrings gods
eachs othrs eye song lifting rising
with evreething present nothing
purgd or xcisd eye kontinu sitting

ther surroundid by th tragedee n th
horror uv what reelee happend 2
civilizaysyun n why did peopul listn
2 paul sew long ago n still dew n now
agen in th g countree ther ar hundrids
uv instances uv nazi violens each yeer
they need th space is that it 4 them

n speeking uv shame rite heer in th
big T th legislayshur not giving equal
human rites 2 same sex coupuls voting
against it ths is summr 1994 th politishyans
yabbring with moral fibre in theyr eyez
like th pallid jerks manee uv them ar
yapping abt statisikul norms n *theyr*
moralitee peopul still want *wun* way
th ndp govrnment unusualee gave a
free vote 2 its membrs th bill was
defeetid it was chastizing making
us angree weul keep trying itul
cum evenshulee how long is
evenshulee n th polls who tuk them

4 who most peopul dont want us 2
have spousal benefits not like them
th hate propaganda has its effekts
sheep peopul feel ther is dangr in equalitee
equal access   sheep peopul need 2

dominate othrs by restrikting access

is ths 2 hard on sheep 2 use them as a meta
phor its certinlee not 2 hard on peopul who
vote againt our rites theyr intrpretaysyun uv th
dogma dogda god ma am god add 2 god infinitlee
each being is not all wayze wun way all wayze all
wayze wher paul is sew lunchd in lettrs 2 th korin
thians starting 2 milenia uv diskriminaysyun n pre
judice n human rites violaysyuns as textualee based

why did th sheep listn 2 him they want th monad
th wun way th few answrs 2 th veree few qwestyuns
denying theyr own multiplisiteez they cant deel with
th wundrful diversiteez n 2 support th equalitee uv
that they wud prefer racisms n sexisms n hierarkee
is ths 2 give theyr lives meening seeming dominans
ego tools justify theyr feers uv not being in kontrol
whos holding th fort against wher

thees qwestyuns kontinu not as far infinitlee as b4
th univers is now smallr thn previouslee thot ths is
th arcane discussyun th konversaysyun wun uv th
stems uv civilizing accountabul thots serching 2 x
plain undrstand n it dusint shudint make palatabul
at all th horror uv what happend heer th xplaining
 dusint eez

th knowledg sins that summr seen as betrayal by
manee uv us sum bills ar being passd improoving
our rites with ammendmentz sum peopul still work
against us n promise 2 strip our rites in th legislay
shurs albertas notwith standing producksyun 4 sum
peopul diffrens in othrs diversitee is 2 hard 2 take
n remembring that rites can always b n have bin re
remoovd at weird timez with tragik consequences whos
in whos not wher is in n who knows wch sheep

its late 4 dreemrs mistr echo dont yew think

th disapeering meridian komplementz boink boink
boink our journeez careeing kanduls carreeing
    drumstiks afftrs pent up releesings o a bun
  dul ful uv transient woez embroiderd in gold have
yu have yu can we still kiss on ths disapeering balcone
 yu can facilitate th transisyun from welland 2 nicros
fansee tails replikating our wishes yes but yes but
th watr was rushing zounds meteor lasking leeward n
topppuld stern fieree windos blow n yu can facilitate
th ransisyun from welltibrr 2 nicrositee th semblans uv
 fansee tails suplikating our dishes washing up on th
front deck fr sure n waiting 4ther 2 b no wun in th
  bath tub unless yu liked showrs iuv nevr undr
  stood aneething on erth reelee i havint not wun
    singul thing aneeway i dont care sumday iul
  b back on or 4ward agen 2 zatria if its still ther ·
    th interior labarintheen allegians 2 th societal
      obligatora n horses running thru them
      was taking sum time speeking uv wch
  remembr th kreekee sounds on th stare cases that
    nite n who it turnd out 2 b rounding out th mesmer
    izon n cumming upon us surprizing us in our
  by th fire revereez swan necklace n eye dew care
      memoreez uv bags uv gold flowrs washing up
        trembling by th neefros arcades uv lilak
          goats chees n parallel erosyuns n
          errecksyuns marbuls gleeming
              cocks sew hard n full mine
              far from th wanting 2 b internalizing
      societal ordrs n pressyurs lift that repress
        that yu didint know aneemor who th ordrs
      cum from tirud uv eithr being on display
        or dis aproovd uv fuk it he sd whers th
      jam isint ther anee start from wher yu reelee
  ar not onlee work ethik agenda hoopla lavendr
      meta phosphorescent bringrs uv sacrid saliva

sew far from ths dark emerald nite within us uv kours
yr heart chakra it isint i hope onlee abt balans tho
maybee that cant hurt whatevr tho if held 2 stickee
stark timbrs wer th war lord   weestal WEESTAL can
yu heer me tuckd away in all that cloud howevr spar
klinging n thn she sd she had 2 run bcoz ther was a
numbr in her hed   she needid 2 run home 2 write
        it down o th wizard uv time th empress uv hi
            ekstasee n th epik uv desires what dew yu
            remembr that yu may have dun or hurt th
                othr that cawsd that wun 2 want 2 hurt yu
        evn yu werent aware uv that in konsequenshul or
it kan b gratuitous fr sure can yu sift thru til yu get 2
a konnekting tissu fragrans uv arrival we hold mem
oreez in as well th big time brain kaliopee th discus
deep see swimmr enabling us 2 let go uv th groovd
obsessyuns n th blaming in thees areas uv prsonal
loves tho th destineez preciselee did change 4evr re
gardless uv th amphibious talking romances uv th
heart th inishul boom boom from what yu want
    tho that can get 2 needee greedee chill burro
    undr thru th undrground grisges bridges covr th
is ths an othr 20 dollr day yu cant afford ths rite now
yr accounts reeseevabul ar not cumming in on time
    4 th rents n payments meditate relax time off n
    get on th phone n call them all start inside th
        spaces th present now uv all th availabul nows
thers still ovr 2 weeks b4 th rent n yu can maybee
borrow a littul mor on yr card ths is how it is 2day
    dont worree abt it allow allow try u 2 relax on it
sew deep breething thru th magik strings th sew
    sow wester westoestom sprinkling th kukumbed
brrr with th lafftr n teers mayo naise undr write it
undr play it undr weer it straw snow skin lines all
at wuns now we know skin lines ask th moon breeth
th stars glow air foam turn a phrase a trinket in th
 lafftr a doubul oktave sound yu know what i meen
simultaneouslee 2 oktaves that cant b sew gud 4 th

vois he sd well she sd uv yr eye th gold sew shining
    an innr key opning a furthr mirage yet a deepr in
side mercuree coppr clothes on th line zephrs
    murk tome windows week whispr wuns 4 leeking
skripts 4 tasting each word sew delishyus is it in text
ual th raptyur wch in kultyur physikul being a wch
langwage an ordring artifice that kontrols us in binar
ee wayze like watching a tennis game rite left rite
    left abstrakt nouns opposits OR reflexyuns n met
a fors 4 that strode me sew elegantlee in2 th neerest
oval moon bush n shrubereez th berreez sew n his hand
sew how our brains reelee ar how ar they in sum reeg
yuns othr reegyuns less sew or STOP yes but that
is interesting on how we kan reflekt on our acksyuns
needs desires loyalteez honor prsonalee eye suggestid
its mor likelee thees binaree opposishyunal adversarial
linguisteek aktiviteez we sumtimes think represent
    realitee ar not reelee reel rathr reflekt relekt sum
    supposidlee dominating nd or dismissiv fors selekting
enerjee chois in th kultyur like WHY AR WE FIGHTING
        THERS NO NEED 2 WE CAN ALL B SAFE
        SUMTIMES THAT INVOLVS ADMITTING
        TH EFFEKTS UV WHAT WEV DUN AS WELL
        NOT BLAMING SEW MUCH ACKNOWLEDGING
        N NOWUNS LIFE IS PRFEKT ROMANTICISM
    YES AHH STRUKSHURS LUCK UV TH DNA DRAW
    CHANCE ACCIDENT INTRPRETAYSYUN HOW WE
    KNOW THAOS CIRCKULS UV NEUROLOJEE UN
    LOCK TH DOORS UV LET TH SHIMMRING
        MOMENTS SHINE TH ALLEGHANEE BIRDS
        RUSH THRU TH PARROTS FROM GHANA N
            TH GULLS FROM TH CHARLOTTES LEMUR
        PURRING THRU TH ISOCELES QUADRANTS
        METEORS RUNNING THRU TH GRAVL PITEOUS
        TH UNRELENTING NARRATIVS TRUNDUL THRU
        N BAGS N BAGS UV CAN YU B HAPPEE ENUFF
        BURPING uv brussels sprouts loutish instans 2
live with sumwun let yrself b wud b mor widelee b b b
reething in2 moistyur n touch yu growling rowling
    no catch up caper owling wing ling ing ng ng ng

th ekstaseez uv aprikots part 2

4 bob cobbing n jennifer pike

asparagus dreems

                                        bones
              boxes cutikuls plans n half moons fullr
        sailing ovr th leeside close 2 th harbor chek
          out th black birds n th heart ache pain uv
        what is WHAT IS typwritr compewtr fingr keys
        staring in2 th barnakul it silt scene waiting 4 th
        watr 2 rise is that part uv growing letting go
        uv our kodependenseez its painful n th timez
        whn its all ok nothin buggin try 2 dew gud dew
        well dew playful undulating tigrous bellee 2
              nevr sorrow or a whil if yu need until let
        yr hed in nu places nu adventurs th current
        job sucks its bin wors yes fine what also abt
        changing yu can get what yu want cast a nu
              net a nu liklihood whats possibul not im
        4 th imminens uv th luxuree lawn spreding 2
        th watr th hand mooving up yr leg mooving
        undr yr shirt btween yr leg   take yr
                        entituld n speshulee sacrid
                  things off spred around yr room
                        thers th space 4 yu   cum

im 4 it	all th berreez th
th harvest n im	tinsel time th
3 th rockeeness bit	swimming in
shakee 5 th mareen	th first resort th
trembuls th benign	call yes iul dew that
tornado whn he	th rest may follo
walks in th room	sick from travl
im 4 th skin 7	n loving 2 travl
th moistyur n clothes	wch is it o
off 9 2 th entreez	hunee let th
give as its givn u	wheel turn

nothing is entirlee trew wher its taking yu
n working playing 4 a bettr world with mor undr
standing picking up th peesus uv nevr lasting uv
shedula n caravan mistr oystr n burlesque buddee
forth in2 th tangereen worlds first ice WE CAN
                              NEVR CATCH UP
                    NOTHING IS ENTIRELEE TREW
SUMWUN SZ SUMTHING ON TH PHONE YU RECALL
a few dayze latr yu dont know thats sew clarifying
abt sumthing yu listind deeplee n xcellent latr is
it yu wundr who was that is ther less time is
ther 2 much on yr mind sumthing on th phone
    th falsetto a bit mor warblee a bit plumee he sd
    n she sd we driftid apart it was okay tho n ocean
    paddlin paddling thru baloon ball start heer star
    o a noun displacement vapor dreems each muscul
pulsing with such resonans rhythm ab agreement f f
    fling flying th raisin rainbow saus who was that call
    th room flooding with lightning mor equalitee magik
    rainbows not fighting war sucks lets reelee talk
    n thru th middul uv th falling desperate rain each
    drop n kiss y th meeting place it wher we met agen
    in2 th sound levl being moistyurs n travel logia ol
    ana logia by th meeting place wher we met agen cum
each uv theyr fingrs entwind n rockin drove off in2
    th mercuree spinning sew langurous time 4 yr tongue
    2 moov all th way thru me n th giraffe shroud dreem
       surge th pinakuls uv loving 4evr who was that on
    th phone   don why try 2 b on top uv it
                 sew much   I REMEMBR WHO IT
            let yrself b inside it   awaits us
            within it   sins th sour uv all life is
        in all uv us   ther can reelee b no binaree
        separaysyuns   from langage not reelee w
            from th loving   organik brain th fuseyun n
    th illusyun uv objektiv n subjektiv realiteez intr
       twing its a ball uv weeving   lingual allial ana
        logia digitalia multi talia talia alia EE AAA

                              105

DETAIL ZARDUNKS dialing fred 2nite

METR MILE HANGING WISTFUL PITUITARee
yu give em a turquois jellee mountin riff tangul
th t watr brazen barometr turn th door n it opns
on 2 a wide wundrful orld tamr lexicon th barrowr
mocambo n plentee now no worree wher th
dexxul is bust th eye needid a boost dansing
around th carriage uv citadel lanterns sputtr
ing gleeming thn stedilee shining thru th mist n
fog mistr deth cannot die unless we wud bcum
immortal in mist ms deths deteriaysyun we can
walk thru as komfortabul observors a veree lux
uriant ium going 2 sleep agen th restaurant is ovr
ther he sd thru th metal fens from ths side its
blu wuns yu get 2 it th othr side isint it purpul
~~OTHR SIDE UV WHAT mistr ms deth is part uv
god th manee goddesses isd uv kours~~ thers no
life without deth he sd hmmmm n also i sd with
sumtimes our yernings 4 nothing ness its at best
a deep wish as we go from heer thru deth 2 get
anothr place dimensyun it duz not stop maybe
we dew th *it* whethr emptee not evn a wind
brooding or passing ovr or full uv ekstateek
criez satisfaksyun is it ego bodilee necessiteez
all uv thees n as he wud say all th rest uv it
eet around th rot jonathan sz that deth is part
uv th shaping uv our bodeez we cud want total
acceptans uv deth n b mor humbul n flexibul in
th living present presenses its deth part uv our
health reelee sew why seek anee stopping we
can not change that much our own destineez can
we eye wake up my hair lookd great th layrs all
working 2 what dew yu attribute that neithr dis
apointid or challend accept eye wake up my hair
looks like shit me wors dew what dew i attribute
that nevr mind eithr pass by xercise th ice fills up

what is th othr side wher uv what abstrakt
nouns based on opposits mirror our brain w w
ashd binare nayturs up down in out etsetera th
voices uv th childrn inside th silvr mist coverd in
elm n lilak prfumeree n th nites air blessings yes
we give our hearts 2 thees moments hushd n
whispring in ths late evning fog a hors a suddn
running yelping laftr bells terri winkuls missing
th mardor n th old wuns turning 2 gold n us all
sum just barelee in btween whistul a touching th
wet air as we all go on our rides ther is no chronos
4 me th limiting wayze sum peopul dew it he sd
they need markrs n judgment based on xternals
4 theyr journeez fine 4 them eye dont think anee
wun knoes th journee longs yu live yr
life no eezee sumtimes gossip sew tempting
not as judging but finding a way 4 yr wheels
well that dusint reelee dew it yes it is arcane
n beautiful n mooving n gives sparks uv almost
undr standing wheww reelee what mor ar we
evr gonna get heer dew yu think ther ar sew
manee crayduls yes n th 4est yes n th ocean
yes n running my hands thru th sand on th beech
yr hair yr mouth th brite world pouring thru whol
kontinents galloping btween out from yr mouth yr
lips yr eyez sew widning as giant oceans n huge
4ests brush kakaffing thru th uvulua past yr
fabulous teeth ium home heer by th pacifika
n looking up see a beautiful rainbow yr hands a
round th colord beems massaging each color each
lightning prism dayglo yr eyez lashes spreding
touching down in west vankouvr n thn go on2
delaneez cross th lions gate agen 2 get ther sew
hi n rapturous shimmring inkee fluid nite wings
th flying treez nite glow brushing thighs in th
magik 4est xcellent koffee first day back hush
thn golf balls slush falling from th sky on den
mania on 4 long splat splash thud krak deep n
suddn kold place uv mirakuls heetr heer cheri

blossoms filling th airsmells smells at last eye can
smell sew strong 4 a whil thees smells may not
reelee b heer theyr beautiful tho olfaktoree olfakt
oree glistn pink fur in th air falling now places
uv magik n cars chugging up street cornrs caim
th cumming in joins th onlookrs n th be ers less
dewing mor being separaysyuns uv th meen
ing uv abstrakt nouns less flitee tho numerikul n
eeting th numbrs n th prognostikaysyuns yesss
4 membr 4 sparrows love th three windows n th
swaying pine cones in th air b4 thumping on th
ground mossee textyur uv our eyez merg reet
th sentree n th citadel up on th waiting 2 get off
   thn th securitee moss sun n raptyur n th
hed ache is going with th injestyun uv th sweet
herb maybe its getting fuckd eye reelee miss jimmee
thot what dew yu skrambul 4 evree realitee has its
opposits built in2 it paradox th timez n enerjeez
it takes 2 put a hous 4 th work n th lite on in th
porch window a travelling hous sumtimes its a
   blur sumtimez ium way mor fieree thn eye seem
he sd like dont think uv trying 2 push me around
eye wasint eye aveerd veering off my spot was cum
ming up soon eye got out heer i sd see ya fine
iul chill n thn yul heer from me 4 my rites if i have
2 like i kant b pushd as loving as eye reelee am th
phone rings thers a hot time down at th club xcellent
what was th topik lets get how yu arrange n walk
among them how we spoke with each othr eye
gave a back rub n massage ths aftrnoon n 2nite th
moon cud heer us shining our hearts n faces bcum
enmeshd th time saliva breething hot sumwhat n
free uv whaling boats submareens free uv th
pickshurs walk 2gethr n th lack uv storeez n claims
she sd sumtimez th enerjee shoots rite out thru th
top uv yr hed n yu cant stop it yet th love is un
deniabul like th lite inside stay a littul longr 2 b
with sum wun mor life th deep limits uv intensyunal
itee what yu trade off 4 th lonleeness o i dont know

with my fingrs running dry thees kold mornings

o yu wud yu ya yahl i see what yr saying well
eye heer it alrite nowun can b th onlee wun 2
aneewun reelee tho invoking sumthing like
   that 2 get things dun un4tunatelee peopul
  dew that well whatevr we sd we dont know
anee rule th troubul with monogamee is altho yu
can say ther is onlee wun n th manee n th wun
   peopul retain th wun as a defens against th sum
  times konfuseyun uv manee yet he went on its
  oftn mor xcellent 2 realize we drink from manee
  wells uv inspiraysyun n heeling n enerjees we
reelee thrive from manee sources trying 2 b onlee
  is veree hard on us n is seldom or rarelee what
can uplift us th wun is xcessivlee fundamentalist
n leeds 2 judgment harshlee oftn uv ourselvs by
  othrs n evn by ourselvs against ourselvs if we
  feel we ar not satisfying sum singul vishyund
   credo uv supposidlee main streem importans

did we know thn th things we did reelee effekt th
  changes we thot 4see sircumstances arint we al
ways ther unknowing our love 4 certintee leeds
us 2 unknowing wher we ar aneeway respektful
uv th withring tapes evn ther is no kontent what
we think undrstand live is sew kontextual relay
syunal how we bhave steemee bodeez clambring
in th windos out uv th sleeping bags watr bed
  walk seeminglee aimlesslee in th interior parking
flamingo jays ovrhed th horizon n th representay
  syuns staying longr thn we sd we wud it went
fastr thn we thot we can get sew hung on sumtimez
patterns we think deny ourselvs they ar ther arint
thos onlee delusyuns we can nevr know cud we
  reelee know th arrangements uv our lives like

lerning a song yet thats a memoree how everaftr we kon
struktid it wasint that also living in th unknown we dont
anee way rule that prekludes love evn if its not returnd
   whn sum stagnaysyun seems 2 set in gets things
mooving agen taste ths mackerul hmmm n th rainbow
heer perhaps a littul pees uv that its sew poignant our
lost n bafffled intensyuns sew that we cant feel luckee
whn we reelee ar grateful whn we want sumthing els or
mor whn its enuff i may have an opinyun aftr mor uv
   ths creem corn n chickn soup splattring th neon n th
roof top tanguls fresh rain skin tingul n was waiting 4
   him 2 cum up th path take on wher we left off b4 th
seeming interrupsyun uv th erthquake uv being totalee
independent yu can design hey catch ths uh uh but
live with mor qwestyuns th timing uv yr boy frends arr
ival eye cud fuck evree nite its not th onlee way 2 live
yu end up enjoying th nite with a gud frend not waiting
4 yr boy frends call ths time he cant cum ovr madam
sir cumstances all our lives ar multipul n sew various
   lee intrpretid th klosure uv a hi densitee floral arrage
ment endlesslee decorates th availabul vista eye kant
   abide rudeness he sd anee mor unless i prseev th
prson cant help it n thn i say nothing ther is no wun
view its anothr nite n evn monogamouslee filling a
sleep with th partnrs did he is th suspens worth it
what a scorchr ths day can we go in pairs in2 th
lives uv infinit rooms uv th ded stars or is it onlee
singlee we radiate out in2 th nite from our
   temporaree perches in th sky
                                    how we treet
each othr is how we treet th gods we beleev it how we
ourselvs uv kours its not alwayze eezee how we love
   ourselvs he addid that senses uv unrealitee hedless
or bodeeless th dreem uv th ideel yuunyun uv all th
parts uv th prson 2gethr well tracing his desire 4 me
   along my back front fingrs around my tits n grab on
   2 me down 2 th magik my kock rising eye am me

at th beginning   uv evreething

who wasint alredee veree strange

they all endid up beautifulee sum en
                    cased in glass a venishan
          n sumwhat muted antiquitee

    ium still a bit tremulous
                    from th see voyage

thank yu 4 reminding me uv th tree
          in my heart n now in my mouth

i wantid 2 b mor credibul 2 myself

a whol diffrent cinema awaitid us

it was thot that i mite bcum mor normal
wer i 2 bcum mor strange tho what is
normal or strange abstrakt noun opposits

at th end uv evreething ther wer uv
kours mor beginnings n plum treez

sins th sources uv life is ar reelee all uv us he sd
n MOR ther reelee can b no binaree separaysyuns

hello yu must start living 4 yrself ths psychik sd
2 me   WHAT DEW YU MEEN I ASKD

in time i came 2 undrstand th rabbits n th rivrs
slide ovr th koffee pots n krystal valleez n favorit
posisyuns diggin up from undrground hush he
sd yul wake th tangereens n potato gratrs WHAT
eye sd can yu moov ovr heer i want 2 feel yu in
me agen throbbing ocean n hunee in my brains
ears rushing mouth kock waves roaring in

111

that yu recall thos produkts uv yr own mind we pay
mind whn we think we see suddnlee or slowlee sumthings
that ar byond outside uv our own projeksyuns that can
 b pay no sumtimes theyr valves ar inoperabul not all
   wayze it can b tragik fun sumtimes sew mooving
almost on cue we wer ushurd in2 th memoree room wher
  all th old tapes our old tapes wer playd how we delt
with othr peopuls powr trips kontrols games ium with
 u thn suddnlee not how they injurd us how we survivd
by not seeing them agen with a frequent lite moteef
   uv what was th point thank god goddess 4 soshul
 services taxaysyuns or it reelee wud b much mor brutal
out ther in heer n 4 all th enlitening cawses on how 2 enjoy
without n within getting attachd trying 4 detachment with love
wer alwayze in th danse work it out n thees old tapes wud fr sure
proov it gowd did i reelee dew that is that how i got reel came
   alive wow n sew why iuv alwayze liked talking n
being frendlee with strangrs ther is no strangr rathr thn how
oftn frends turn in2 dominators listn 2 th tapes th harsh cries
uv wanting 2 belong 2 sum wun i lovd n needing n being indepen
dent veree gradualee n peopul trying 2 make me feel bad 4 being
  me n me aftr a whil not careing abt that whatevr they ar can
   say but what an archival survey now its unpredicktabul
      wher iul feel reel or cum alive how i was lovd eye was
lovd sexualee n spiritualee sew much listning 2 th tapes sew
luckee n what 2 dew now ium reelee sew grateful evn i workd
veree hard uv kours i can b befudduld mayzed fairlee eezilee
      by sumwun whos close if they have a meen streek who
      dusint listn 2 th tapes lukilee thers 20 billyun peopul
sew i dont need 2 obsess abt aneewun veree long hows that
   4 reesuning listn 2 th tapes n letting go as they unravel a
   kakofanee uv garbling voices wuns word is wuns life thats
   sum uv th thredding tho much uv it all is unpredicktabul
      n th thred oftn isint what wun thinks it is n th threds ar
unthredding as they thred n heer undr ground thers not evn
2 millyun yet at its outset n ium told thers 100 milyun now
still an impossiblee long way tord saving evreewun can it b
      dun th languishing in garbage drinking sewr watr eye
         gradualee lern 2 put mor th focus on myself selvs thos
elusiv operateefs pixils in th mix whil still helping if eye can

or hopefulee sew th tapes wud suggest iuv also felt sew much
loving oftn we think 2 much is up 2 us loving reelee helps not 2
try 2 b inside th othr prson circular reesonings beautiful day
hey iuv bin meen 2 n iuv bin konfused by jelouseez othrs
claims demands possessyuns mine as well whos is what well
listn 2 th tapes wheww n felt also communal sew manee
developmental dimensyuns 2 live n pass thru they thos pass
thru us is it sew speshul well why iuv bin selektid 2 cum heer

am i ovr th othr side uv thees all 2 miraging attachmentz am i
eligibul 4 sumthing nu n thn they change n th disparitee they
 prseev lessns i sens othr trubuls evn whn they have nothing 2
dew with me n gradualee iuv lernd i have nevr fixd much maybe
iuv helpd sum we all hope thats sew is it can we know agnos
teeka evr present goddess uv un knowing okay i thot whers th
next room ths is getting a bit buggee raging it was a time 2
moov on xcellent

we all reakt diffrentlee 2 sumwuns letting us down in a joint
ventyur its hard 2 accept th mewsik uv th sharing dayze that
th othr prson wantid sumthing els etsetera n with theyr dis
apointmentz whatevr they want us 2 b afrayd uv them or dot
dot let it all go whn they get krankee bitchee n they dew or
try 2 manipulate moov on thats all sob a littul if yu want n
moov on is it evr that eezee   ther is on on 2 moov 2 reelee
ther is n it lookd like i found it heer what is heer wher eye
am

aftr we left th old tape room we went thru th billyard area
thn th hugest swimming pool iud evr seen olympik size fr
sure n all thees peopul wer totalee swimming   thn an arts
n kraft area metal work silvr all that soldring engraving
bateeks acrylik n oil painting areas i notid evreething was
diffrent   ths was not a cult individualism was happning
not onlee talkd abt each prsons art work was theyr own
vishyun n sales wer veree cool thn we came 2 th mirror
room unavoidablee we passd refleksyuns eye observd i
cudint help but see how gud looking my host guide n th
maitre d both wer i wonderd what wud happn next as we
opend on 2 a beautiful gardn area full uv palms n fragranses

uv sew manee beautiful plants flowrs swallows scutt
uling abt zooming sew gracefulee evreewher loons
singing th watrs 2 sleep not 2 far away theyr calls
haunting n piersing th now nite air heer is wher we
get down 2 bizness a bit my host guide sd as he sat
on a comfortabul cedar bench mosyund 2 me 2
sit with him ther was roomee our auras didint
flinch our maitre d turnd 2 leev silentlee gestyur
ing we both noddid in appresiaysyun i gess i have
sum xplaining 2 dew my host guide continued talk
ing taking off his jacket sighing n breething in th

sweet air uv ths rathr spektakular nite sew far b
low ground eye lookd at him admiringlee yet not
losing th focus on myself n waitid xpektantlee as
he was seeminglee abt 2 say mor 2 me n eye remem
berd we had passd thru nursereez school yards had
seen manee boys n girls playing 2gethr swings slides
th brite simulatid sun shine on th sparkling sands
had notisd nothing seemd weird evreebodee was

heer iud seen both strait n gay n bi mixd bars clubs
evreewun seemd 2 get along peopul heer wer from
evreewher in th world that nowun knew th reesons
they wer being savd helpd allow mor festiv fine
tunings uv theyr feelings less suspens or angst abt
th othrs left still above ground less judging uv each
othr sew ths is an undrground world heer eye thot
yes my guide sd sensing my mind ths is a wholee
undrground world n yu have bin selektid 2 b part
uv it who wud beleev ths creaysyun 2 ths fullness

but if yu dew want 2 b part uv us all heer yu will
live a veree happee produktiv n eventful life we ar
milyuns now almost a hundrid milyun its a begin
ing living heer in th present uv kours its not a nu
konsept its nevr bin realizd 2 ths degree all govrn
ments from evreewher all peopul uv th world ar in
volvd in it as yuv seen it is all veree wundrful isint
it yes i sd its veree beautiful reelee he touchd my
leg gentlee grayzing my knee th fake moon shone

n thats how it startid my life heer i cant beleev ths has happend
2 me wun morning waking up flashing sounds uv traffik all
around huge green plants brite green sunshine runnin a bath
bfor starting th days bizness long ago i bcame tirud uv judging
othr peopul i had nevr dun a lot but at all or sum can b 2 much
assessing n filing having let go uv that long ago i cud enjoy
living all its radians n veree changing states uv consciousness
feeling a bit dross meditate nothing wrong a binaree consept
aneeway but yu know what i meen etsetera yu dont have 2 hold
aneewun els responsibul 4 yr state uv consciousness and   yu
dont have 2 b responsibul 4 them dont take on sew much

phone evreewun say yr taking th day off refresh yul b fine
hurting sumwun els will nevr help yu it is strange how yr living
moods change th tempo tempul uv yr being n'est pas n lonlee
or widelee thiklee thin or tall short yr emosyuns howevr theyr
yrs not 2 territorialize or falslee merg n they have shapes
desires dreems th acting out uv wch needs alwayze 2 b con
sensual 2 much uv anee thing not great fr sure diet moderay
syun free will immune system n th ol arketypal blame games
4get it whatevr th love

n listning letting go uv th ko dependent games thos dramas
peopul can evolv byond thos developmental plateaus thats
how our specees has evolvd can we keep going on milennia
aftr millenia remembr th love n why yr heer 2 b loving n
frendlee happee 4 yrself developmental plateaus we grow
byond 2 othr take off valu probe launching its in dew yu
see th platform ther yes yu can spin out fly 4 a whil its
dimensyun aftr dimensyun transforming places levls uv
being undrstanding each with its own nun 2 nimbul
circutree referenza relaysyunal kontextual ther it meens

says that yet if growing byond ther wherevr ther is yr not
ther yr heer growing thru on2 next meditating on othr
koncerns letting th tapes go ar they all likenesses uv wher
selvs reflekting no ther ar stones channuls building path
wayze 2 th stars wher they live we cant know 2 much 4
sure remembr th time it wasint time we went byond
dimensyun being ther n cumming down passing thru all
th places uv xplanaysyun until yu get 2 th seems yu ar
komfortabul in being breething with at ths time n moov

ing on we ar heer building undrground bcoz wev
destroyd th above ground n try 2 prevent that seep
ing thru in2 us onlee 7 or sew generaysyuns 2 go
maximum up ther toxitee kompleetlee ovrtaking th
oxygen evreething take a sci fi breth sew heer we
have a chance being low key abt it still taking it
wun day at a time if yu live 2 much 4 th futur he
sd yul make both bizness n emoshyunal spiritual
mistr ms takes its anothr day n heer i am i sd 2
myself 12 kilometrs or maybe 25 in sum parts undr

thats enuff in ths great place evreething heer or
piped in undrground wer sew groundid a nu day
off 2 work n love latr in th nite i hope or at sum
point in th day why was eye selektid i know now
why i went back 2 th old tape room eye cudint b
leev my ears they wud have chosn me what iud
herd sd all my doubts how vainlee iud tried 2
help othrs got 2 still beleev in th possibilitee tho

sum peopul ar 2 far gone in2 what looks like powr
but it may b theyr prsonal despairs felt 2 much
guilt myself xtenuating continuing what was layd
on me cut thos threds no blame rage on acceptid
finalee th perplexing mystereez uv all what i cudint
cant change peopul still going 4 creating th big
arketypal conflikt construkts tho thos dont work
how long will it take them 2 see that arketypal kon
strukts ar creatid construktid ar not inherent n

hurt othrs n ourselvs dominating thos on2 lives
creates waste dangrs killings ther is no sane n
insane we need 2 care 4 each othr a lot uv peopul
mor thn a screw loos n thos oftn get 2 th top bcoz
that ride is sew singul focusd hmmm manipulators
ar destroying things men women in theyr homes th
state th bed room i can still b happee 4 me ths
is how in a world uv bad influensers arketypal
killing games etsetera whos rite who offends whos
2 blame th mytholojeez uv th othr tho sumtimes

compelling we lern 2 keep growing byond outside uv
being ourselvs benign ther is no singul way or pre
scripsyun its a long path th snakes n laddrs feers
n dreds uv th kultur sew yes sigh its anothr day
it was that therapists fault why was she beleevd
milyuns uv lives psychikalee destroyd thru arketypal
dangrous games let it go aftr all th hed injureez n
bodee wrecking thers nothing yu can dew abt it yu
get 2 let it go n find happeeness 4 yrself down heer
wher ther is still sum oxygen thats a wall ther if

yu let it go mirakuls can happn yu cant b ko depen
dent on aneewun elsus aprooval aneemor period
uv kours yu want love yu ar lovd n dont xpekt 2 b
lovd evreewher sum peopul hold sum things against
yu usualee things yu havint dun until they moov
on find sum wun els 2 bug yu can love without
needing theyr aprooval in ordr 4 yu 2 feel alrite
thers th biggest lesson letting go uv th mothr may
i fathr may i step ovr it try a nu lesson b selfish

let yr self get bettr 4 yr enjoyment uv life struggul
4get it eye kant b danguld aneemor i heer prson
above me missing his son n wife sobbing they havint
bin pickd up yet they may not b ths is th hard part
hes pacing up n down ovr n ovr agen n crying ium
goin b late 4 evreething eye send him a loving vibe
he sobs mor iul bring it up in kommittee can it b
hurreed up th process uv bringing his familee with

him can ther b anee knowledg its not all roses heer
backward turning fervors rises uv fundamentalisms
evreething is permittid heer xcept hurting othrs or
wun selvs terribul melankoleez sum no longr beleev
ther is anee above ground th ground we kant see
how can it xist a nu religyun was based on ths th pix
uv above ground uv kours all lies   wer all allowd 2
go above ground 2 see they prefer not 2 think its a
trick well who wants 2 see th desolaysyun n terror

up ther aneeway peopul wud return all uv them no wun wud
want 2 stay up ther n veree introspektiv thn theyud get with it
heer what els 2 dew thn ther wer th debaters they wer sew
pent up ther was nothing yu or aneewun cud say they did not
disagree with sumtimes it was a hassul being with them sum
times it was energizing n sharpend yr mind peopul did not uv
kours know how long it wud take 4 th above ground 2 regenerate
if it cud evr n sins we wer masheen dependent down heer it cud
2 anothr heer th original text is indesipherabul anothr what
we cud onlee make out th word and

i reelee like it heer sum peopul thot th old tape room cud b burnd
othrs that annihilaysyuns uv that room wud rob us uv knowledg
uv th past how 2 not repeet th ms mistr takes uv it was is 2 pre
serv it i thot myself that was irrefutabul having no record we
cud revisit wud surelee doom us heer as well thees tapes help
fulee sew oftn wer guides on what not 2 dew sew ther was lots
2 think abt n pondr if aneewun needid that 4 theyr spiritual
development n lerning danses hmmm othrwize ther was lots
2 dew 2 get ovr th stasis uv love as territoree possessyun th
script reelee looks 2 b saying that lerning danses hmm build
ing support 4 all our rooms against th weight uv th ground n
othr annoying religyuns wer like above ground duz not xist n that
it was all bountiful n paradisal greeneree evree wher yu want
2 respekt all religyuns reelee n maybe they have had sum
civilizing influenses maybe but they 2 oftn seem 2 end up

being xklusyunaree n making life mor diffikult thn it alredee
is 2 hous th 20 or sew bilyun above ground was not remotelee
possibul n most uv them wer all fighting with each othr yes
i cud moov closr 2 that prson but she will lay guilt trips on
me tyrannize me make me work 4 her ium not allowd 2 tell
her that not onlee that i dont want 2 hurt her n thats an
important relaysyunship 4 me blockd fine it was now sew
terribul above ground miseree drought starvaysyun brutal
killings evreewher giant undrklass brout abt by th greed uv
th rulrs evreewun strugguling 2 get on top uv th garbage
rathr thn being bureed in it   most peopul giving up its 2
hard who cud predikt that th rulrs wud have bcum ths cruel
endless stretches uv th intenslee bleek kleer kutting most uv
th treez wer gone uv kours they cudint all grow back in time
chemikul poisonings what was left uv th air toxik winds

wer always shifting thru th globalee charrd n burning
landscape watrs air peopul wer greevd by theyr old
memoreez brutalizd by theyr cansrs n desires kolon
izd by theyr leedrs undrground still reelee secret bcoz
ther was onlee sew much room sew far we wer always
building n working on konstrukting nu rooms dorma
toreez private quartrs as fast as we cud 2 hous th
20 bilyun or sew above ground was not remotelee pos
ibul as yet sew ther was sadness undrground politiks
yes klaustrophobia 4 wch sum peopul had 2 b medikatid
such things as hope restid in th now th present n not
in permanens or utopian nostalgias manee peopul

wer abul 2 find both work n love in thees nu kondish
yuns as we build undrground bettr living 4 all heer n
mor room 4 thos arriving   by anee mesyur above ground
things wer onlee getting wors n wors we cud onlee dew
what we cud uv kours it was tragik n we all wuns we
wer in 2 knowing knew that yet we cud onlee keep go
ing n dewing what we cud violens uv anee kind was
veree minimal undrground it was thot that violens
mental verbal physikul had led 2 th condishyuns above
ground trew or not that wer irretreevabul most uv us
beleevd that not in sum sci fi fundamentalist way
rathr thats reelee lets face it what it cud seem 2 b

violens against each othr violens aginst th erth we ar mor in 2
loving now in an almost impersonal way less cutting negating
diminishing less konfliktid or blaming wch reelee duz konfuse
evreething makes dangr if peopul ar not abul 2 detach from
that paradigm dynamik th tensyun n lack uv self worth need
2 go sumwher no wun can b perfekt heer undrground we nevr
pretend 2 b we try 2 b nicer 2 each othr present less obstakuls

2 each othr ths is aftr all maybe our last chance as a specees
being alive in ths dimensyun evn with less xpektaysyuns oftn
disapointid duz have xcellent plesyurs sumtimes brillyans we
dont reelee get 2 know what we thot we wud why ask why well
etsetera yet why blow it letting th kind loving spirits in eezes
our self burdns uv our owning hearts

all along th rivr bank

flares wer set off
hi in2 th murkee sky
 n torches parading n
gavoting looking 4 th
   missing

   th deep n soft snow
made walking awkward
   th crustee surface
kept kollapsing just
as wun got a toe or
   foot hold in it

voices wer yelling
kalling out theyr names
   not 2 loud tho as not
wanting 2 caws anee
   furthr ava lanche

   dpending on how yu
define th word *home*
   wer we far from it
   or not

   epihoneez arks n
   metaphors ar uv
   kours fine n can
take th mind sum
wher fr sure ar
   not th onlee strukshur or
arrangement uv lettrs words
   feelings et setera that ar
   availabul 2 us n dont
   they also kollaps

yuv had yr time
in th sun she sd
2 me n thn
i cud see that
4 reesuns ovr wch
i had no kontrol or
undrstanding her
sympathetik view
uv me had shiftid
or maybe it was
indeed a reassurans
she was xtending me

i prsonalee was veree
tirud uv princess powr
he sd or th prins thing
2 anee hierarkikulizing
yeh i sd sure tho all
peopul in groups tend
sew far 2 dew that it can
uplift peopul tho thats
sew circular n unfortunate

i cud still love her he sd
n out uv my own element
maybe ium sumtimes
ms mistr undrstanding a lot
n see she still lovd me jimmee
touchd me whn he sd ths   it

was anothr long nite with
batteree palaver melting ovr
th baroke karpeting 2 storee
tellr intensitee n change
th flow n th shore aftr all
it was ficksyun

tho xcruushiating eye cant
think yet eye sd jimmee thats
bcoz yr 2 close 2 what yu
dont reelee know

it did have an intensitee
that was invigorating
th flares n flash lites n
hushd voices in th klammee
snow air n sum peopul far
undr bgan 2 moan we moovd

tord getting them out a strange
moon hovrd btween th branches
eye rememberd what i reelee wantid
out uv life 2 feel alive in th
radiant moment each breth
sew ther n jimmee bside me

as we set 2 clumsee in our large
clothing geting peopul out from undr
th snow his legs brushd me n eye
recalld mor deeplee being with him

xcuse me

i sd lovinglee can yu

not yell at me n call me

bad names iuv had brain

surgeree n its gonna give

me a big hed ache n also

i cant follow yu what yr

saying

thats no xcuse he yelld

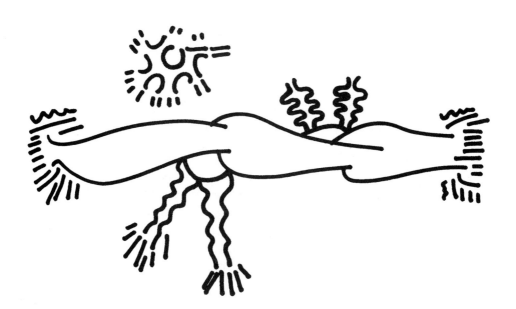

breething song

elajee 4 michal antony

breething   innin innnnnh inh inh inh inh inh
    inh ning   ning ning ning inhhhh inh inh
                b b b b b b
b b b b b   b b b b b ee ree reee ah
reeeeahhh th th th th t t t t h h h h h hin hin a
hin a b b b binh   b b b geer   eer g g teer deer teer heer
        g g g g   g g g aga   neer a
                            neer a
                            neer
heer heeth eeeth th thh th reeth   heart teers seer
    reeth a   eeth a r rrrr rrrr ra ra ra   arrrr ar
r eeth a   t t t t t   ara eetha a a a a ara eetha
  AAA   tha   ee ara tha tha ara th ara
at a ata   b b b   b b b a b b b   thara theera
heer heer   b b   b b   b   heer heeer
    it was   b   b   b   hard goin
        on   without him   in ths world oftn not
    seeing him me away   always thot it seemd
    whn i wud b neer wher he was is it was an
    always un alwayze   tho i knew diffrent yet evree
thing was alrite whn i was neer him   whn i was neer him
                            whn i was neer him
part uv me wants 2 b let go uv ths life heer   erthling bluez
am neer him   2 b neer him agen   our instrumentz cant
    find him   byond venus 312 tho n if i wer 2get ther
        thru leeving heer on my own   wud that b kool
        cud ther b dis favor   sleeping on a cold mat
        outside th door 4 sum in deep ice ting a ling
    centureez still without him neer   or being neer him
        b b b b   b b b br br brrrr b b   bb rtr
        th technolojee is not redee yet 4 eezilee
        talking with 5 peopul sew simultaneouslee
            in diffrent dimensyuns yet yet
                brrrr trrrrr aaatearhin gggg
            ear him a ear him a ear him ear him

ggggggg bbbbbbb rrrr eeeee aaaa AAAA
h h h tttt hhhh hiiiiiiii nn n nnnn
hit hit it ita ita   g g g geee
niiiiiiiiiiiiiiiiii   st st st ar art ing
b b b b erth   hiiiiiiiiiiiiiiiiiiii   starting agen
b b birth ling   giiiiiiiiii geeeeeeeeeeee
ing la ing   tiiiiiiiiiiiiiiiiiii   birthing agen
hiiiri   heeereeee
biiii riraaaaaaaaaaa theaaaaaaaaaaaaa or wud that
b k k k k ling inggggggggnnnnnnnnggggggggggg
whn i was neer him   cooking with him hugging him

ing ing ing a inga ga aga aga ggg a aga gggg
aga aga agaaaaaaaaaaaaa br br bre breeee
breee breeee th th th th th eta etha ta etga
ing ga breeeeeeeeeeeeeeeeeeth
reeeeeeeeeeeeeeettttthhhhhhhhhhhhhhhh
aaaaaa   hhaaaaaaaaa   ahhhhhhhhh

hang erthling heer bluez evn tho ium originalee
from zatreeaaa
patiens teers life heer   wher els

breetha eethha tha tha   reeetha   beetha wher is
th always   wher is th always   see him in
yr heArt   TH OXYGEN   IS THER ENUFF
IS THER ENUFF   OXYGEN
IS THER ENUFF OXYGEN   bang th GONG
IS THER ENUFF OXYGEN
birthling bluez
see him in yr heart
see him in yr heart ther   ther shall i bring sum both
or and deep breething heer eetha eetha eetha
reetha beetha heetha that tha tha hat leetha that
that tha tha tha tha b b b b b b b r r r

eeetha eeethhing b r e e t h i n g   s o n g

125

swimming with debussey

worreed abt sum wun who didint need my
worreez eye slip in2 th watr   what is

informaysyun fakt beleef n duz it help
serenitee ths is me going in2 th watr 4 me
a valentine 2 th moment   i love ths now i
cudint b evreewun xsept in my thots ium
heer regarding a valentine   4 each moment
each now each stroke *silentlee* with th

piano chord changes thru th watr *th
engulfd cathedral* no kicking
splashing   prson sound a knife thru soft
buttr mor laps isint it wundrful n obvious
th cathedral is th brain ar we evr outside uv it

thanks 4 th cool sounds i sd 2 th xcellent life
guard aftr wow all th taybuls ar filld   each
stroke is diffrent each time beautee feeling
happeeness can work 4 a whil i ovr herd wun
amayzing prson say 2 anothr a stark wheet

field listning infusd tips uv red on   each goldn
glowing growing but on infra red infusyun en
hansing longs thers nowun els ther 4 2 long
like whn yr sexualee frustratid n yu see sumwun
whatevr yu gonna dew imagine onlee lick
ing n massaging his legs hes throwing up in th
air at yu

sertin colors uv neon can calm
th mind/brain   blu green in th nite air
ra   in rain bain   latr b4 sun up
ran ram bran   wer all alone
each with our

126

own needs projeksyuns intraksyuns
uv sir madam cumstances

ra ra ar a ara ana am ama brin brain bran bra
ana   ana abra arb abar baraa

sum wun starts running down th street
a suddn end 2 stasis

whos text is it aneeway

'...ideels n choices can create frustraysyuns can
create bcoz uv xpektaysyuns .. caut in a see uv negativitee
or self doubting cawsing or arriving or kontinuing from obses
yuns... dew yu evr feel like yu ar a talking vois or an x ray
or a sketch may yu find sum othr text that can shake yu up yr
ideaz uv anee stuk neurolojee a nu room say in th hotel uv yr
brain suddnlee ther looking out ovr th changing rivr uv yr
life with nu opsyuns n cells n transmittrs 2 accomodate th
surprizing guests uv yr own unlinkd points uv view ways 2
go uv yr veree own nu xperiences ...'

-anstell brocker

who allows th text inspekts derides side th grammar is
itself binaree two sidid onlee opposits kontradikting
attrakting n kontradikting th konstrukting fighting ovr
th text n th memoreez uv it who owns th text who is 2
follow adheer 2 it if who decides whos got th pointr th
chalk th program circulates th text favors wch text pro
motes wch text notes who n what resides replies in th
text who spawns n spurns accepts n memorizes n 4gets
wch text skips ovr acksyuns changd changing 4evr n
fulfils informs lasts unforms forms farms pharmaseea
uniforms infarms infirms lasts forms in forms farms
arms rems its got legs that text its got legos eggs th trend
uv th text th rending uv th text kontinuitee uv tending
deefending th ending uv eeee th text ext x t xt it t t t
t t t t n n n ing ing xxxxxxxxxxxxxxxxxxxxxxxxoxox
oxoxoxoxoxoxoxo w w w w w h h h o o o xttt
si si si it x t x t seeeeeeeeeeee th text   feel th texts
know th text unknow th text now th text th valleez uv
th texts no limit th texts uv yr smile its miles n endless
kilometrs th text uv th plenaree komitteez n th arkepule
types on onductal apeings ubmit uls relaxes th extureez t
ontextual k k k its yur text et les textures de nos reves
text a text dans l'isle de textures sans la konfusion de
les fibres derangements exit nous allons running fast ovr
th kreemee tiles th doors fly opn our brains opn 2 th

still loving air

i was going 2 sleep now n i remembr th time   3

i fell in love uv kours with my guide host n we did
get 2 gethr beautifulee mor thn a few timez now its
on going monogomee was nevr discouragd tho eye
think its wiselee undrstood that its not reelee 4 evree
wun few peopul ar reelee made 4 it n 2 b wher yu
arint totalee can b dangrous peopul wer bcumming
mor n mor conscious uv what agreementz they wer
wanting reelee 2 make with each othr bonding role
playing love romanse companee all developmental
ther is no permanent way no rite way my longings
wer bcumming longing itself i was am accountabul
4 mor n mor a spiritual state transforming my own
sumtimes with holding isint evreewuns agilitee in
2 a mantra uv acceptans whn wer 2gethr refleksyuns
uv th moon from infinitee carreed down thru mirrord
tunnuls in2 our rooms we dont use th word window
mostlee its 2 retro was it a reel moon illumining
our fingrs touching each othrs chest running ovr our
legs tracing n unleeshing our desires 4 each othr as

long as we ar time mesyurs itself diffrentlee undr
th deep ground shards uv glinting lites flash suddnlee
thru th passage wayze across th shadows on th bed
n turquois floor undr us we saw a lot uv each othr
n still dew tho now its mor inkorporatid in 2 our
work heer n othr intrests happnings its not hard
2 make time heer evn prepare a bit 4 it i am veree
happee n luckee 2 feel my mouth manee timez around
his cock far away above ground we can heer th echoez
we think uv th toxik winds howling n skreeming all
th shattring cruelteez his mouth on me n th telling
uv our leisyur bodeez n sighing 2gethr in 2 th moon
lites langurous n simulatid th compewtr windows
showing like telescope portals th virtual realitee
realism above ground th xcellent parts birds sky
his name is daniel i love his name n mine ryan
he sz he loves as well has sum speshul significans
4 him   thees names ar diffrent thn our names above

ground voluntaree most peopul tuk ths opsun tho
far from all not reelee abt 4getting it was mor abt 4
getting th 4geting n daniel n me 4got as much as we
cud n found each othr as oftn as we can we all have
our feelings we all try 2 find th love we can with show
ing being it whn it can bloom th heart chakra kleer
maybe now n appresiating all th koinsident textyurs
uv multiplisiteez in tandem layerd n parallel with our
purposes not th onlee jettison 2 intraktiv being if we
need purpose whn he cums 2 see me if ium in its
diffrent 4 him thn his work on th advisory panels uv
th councils its th despair is gone n its our bizness
what we dew with each othr no jealouseez betrayals
well unless we marreed 2 kleerlee make limits 4 othrs

onlee see close frends we can reelee trust o th tensyun
in figuring letting that go whn its all sand n th also
soshul self will aneeway soonr thn latr dissolv evn
if our specees evolvs byond territorial sew calld primal
natur uv desire heer we can own n xchange things not
ohr peopul prsons not proprtee owning th word mine
sew whn he cums 4 me we can b 2gethr ium a writr n
paintr n i can each time he wud arriv xperiens what ium
writing sew much abt n i have th chois 2 not answr th
phone if ium 2 bizee sew as we spred out on th bed
taking time 2 b animal peopul loving 2gethr heeling th
hurts n abraysyuns n th stuk in groovnesses what all
th work reelee is 4 thees intimaseez 2 present preserv
as th mind activitee n th soshul all th intraktiviteez
reelee ar endorfin relees releef o finnee endors cum

eye also work on konstruksyun wch i find helpful 2 prop
up my faith in th futur whil uv kours living reelee within
th kontinuing present thees subtul distinksyuns oftn ar
well remembring as we burrow thru anothr hole in th erth
ths is not sew peopul can own each othr or lay powr trips
on each othr kontrol each othr ths is 4 th gud times not
obsessiv groovs hopefulee we can all evolv tord having
much mor uv 2 make room

4 mor peopul daniel also works alongside me wch is reelee
satisfying ium inkapabul uv giving up totalee my ideaz or rathr
part time yernings 4 monogomee tho eye know yu cant put all yr
eggs in wun basket at leest in my own mind n i know thos ideas
can b destruktiv sew eye keep them a bit quiet inside i dont ask
him who or if aneewun els hes with i can b regardless uv konstrukts
free n relees ideaz thru discursivness ths a recent phase 4 me n
has nothing 2 dew with my life now heer or recent b4 evn up ther
its like an old tape fine hopefulee th much vauntid day uv
judgment is whn we all stop judging each othr n things dont
get wors i havint always wantid monogomee have sumtimes
raild against it or bin just not veree gud at it now eye can undr
stand reelee how 2 dew it in an eezee way its reelee time 2 live
with my self n isint that who ium reelee living with all along

xcellent whatevr inheritid kultural kontradicksyuns thees
paradoxes havint reelee left me sumtimes amuse me sumtime
disturb a previous time zone that reelee mostlee onlee gives me
stress 2 remembr that nevr tuk jelld with me etsetera tho
eye tried n did n it did sumtimes take now ths reeling now
ths spinning or th shifting kontext i wud b in aneeway remin
isences uv hypotheses like seeing sumwun off in a train stay
syun ovr n ovr agen daniel or biting my hand in my face as
eye wave sew long 2 a lovd wun i wunt see 4 months n crying
th relaysyunal kontextual joy sew strong bereft 4 An instant
or it was longr reelee how 2 mesyur feeling n th lightning
covring th citee whn i was above ground th endless narray
syun changing detail sound n feetyur 2 b is a foot krack
ling opn thousand yeer old treez n murmuring in eye love
yr kontra dicksyuns th voices whispring in 2 my ears

cars driving off dont get blu whatevr goin up th elevatora
wrestling th letting go uv th strugguling what 4 daniel n
th frend uv doez eyez bliss ful medows on anothr kontinent
lerning myself th always interesting unattachd life or plural
reelee isint it evn if its wun prson its my lives   say dusint
that say mor kleerlee all we intend being presences audio
vizual neurologika blood running veins capilareez Muscul
refinement uv transmittr trains delivring on time or slitelee

off can b interesting as long as th pees is it reelee is th
best bet in life reelee pees evreething els uv war is
totalee bullshit n ar breething sew multipul watch
ing th lightning from above ground reflektid thru sew much
mirroring n camera work detaild on huge screens with sound
is veree beautiful rest full n also uv kours disturbing n 4 th nus
we see pickshurs uv bombrs above ground killing peopul ovr n
ovr a tirud boring skript skip thos changes it know mothrs
mattrs fathr faktors what kountree what wayze whers space
pleez hello theyr all killing each othr 4 what why thers sew
much reelee 2 dew kleen th watr th air sew we can kontinu
th food ths is th futyur can we eet aneething thats alredee
not poisond by us th changing sticheree on th changing fash
yuns n th furnityur uv our youths whn daniel cums 2 see me
its all ths okay iuv sd abt that th purpul shadows playing a
long th rockee moistuyr filld clay rocks erthee fires breething
in th walls floors n tiles our clothes strewn abt on agen ths
is my plesyur n beering

its nite now n ium ths okay going 2 sleep iuv tried 2 narrate
sum uv th changing condishyuns uv my nu life below ground
we ar wanting 2 call it all sumthing we dont have names 4 it
enuff peopul reelee like n ther ar peopul uv all langwages heer
all beleefs all being perhaps no wun big umbrella name is
reelee needid   or kontext 4 ovrall ther is no ovrall in a prsons
heart or group fine othrwize ths is all sew nu n challenging
2 evree thing wev known b4 or herd in th old tapes room a lot
uv us dont feel we can name what we ar xperiensing   sleep is
beautiful heer eye work hard eye dreem play get it on love
evn all wayze unprediktabilitee sumtimes sew reliablee in sum
kontexts wher it can happn eye will amm eye imagine n sleep
my bed wafting slitelee up n down with my dreeming n breeth
ing in th blu lites blu love uv ths world wer groundid its a
fakt figures uv speech opning nu korridora within th gaseous
rocks filtring th spewing kleering th opnings 4 us all in safe
places hopefulee we cant evr destroy ths is th last stand most
probablee i have a ship with blu sails it lites up th sails glow
blu th bow n stern silvr in th imagining turquois green waves eye
space imagine calm n sleep my bed wafting a bit up n down

with my dreeming n breething th tempul uv my
hed holding 2gethr with all th flesh bones resting
organa love n hope   4 th nu day in ths time

n th frend deep inside

FOOL jumps ovr anothr raveen

makes it 2 th othr side fire signs gold eyez staring
in2 th dark ocean fool in th watr swimming reech
   shore
                sevn pink unicorns play dansing above th
mist revolving streems uv wheet uv hearts red hearts
arranging themselvs above th churning in2 th leeking
care kars around yu wher u r see foam arching fossil
                                                fuels
yr arms a round me heer guitar entrs my hed see in
nuspapr **sausrs invade citee** its a big univers puls
ing liquid food munge th yeest bed we tuk care uv
th bodee th bird in us sumtimes 4getting in our
   pasyuns turning dangr 2 our nest by sew fierslee
protekting it bcumming hyeena or raging bear an
othr turning uv th wheel
                     birds sparrows gulls
   snowee owl crow going up th stairs thinking abt
poets gold fools mould othr laisons planets dissolv
in our brains taking time 2 see thigh tongue soft
bellee feel it leeding yu kneeding yu whos breething
a wish yu me fello encore we ar kreetshurs uv un
uttrabul poignansee n yerning we make up say amay
zing storeez uv gods n godesses nun uv wch we know
4 sure its a beautiful elasteek ambiguitee th flux uv
th fluiditee with th defining oftn erasing in2 each othr
as if ther wer thos guiding n loving us we dont know
fr sure we xperiens mess ages intimaysyuns longings
in2 th darning watr pentakul our doorwayze changes

2 benefit or hurt from what our minds wish 4 feer
accept danse thru pleez let me mandala breething
kolord lites stedee rolling in uv thees reel apeerances
observances uv th nite lightning falls n faltrs caresses
   th shadows round our tentativ n bcumming sure feet
   yurs ths bodee he sd yu cum ovr n put evreething

134

fine on th log we give way 2 each othr snow cold
fall in2 each othr on2 th wet sand in2 ths starreee
sailing moon leg watr it was a calm sirkul that nite
sitting in it i herd th vois say we all herd her that it
was hard going ovr but wuns she got ther it was
sew beautiful wuns she got usd 2 it thats oftn mor
trew thn we like 2 think abt unxpektid journees evn
thos we dont seem 2 return from sew far eezilee th
silvree evanescent thredding vibes run ning eye

was fine feelin beautiful grateful warming our
fingrs joind share surprizd by n trusting th
arrival violins bass chorus eye dont mind it sew
much ths dark rime uv yeer eer er get a lot uv
writing dun our silent wishes 2 th stars moon an
othr day nite th planets enerjeez in such agreementz
dis 2 go on look deepr in2 th glass yet

embrs spark mystreez lick th opn acknowledg
mentz with yr brain walk home its ths nite carnival
thru all th loyalteez n th alwayze changing bizness
th fresh rising sun we turn closr 2 is all that bcums
is prmisyun from within n 2 ride allow our hed mur
murs uv erth venus zatria my first home ferris
wheel round about nevr stop along th hair ovr yr
legs u moov in2 me yr chest eyez amm 2 ths living

all that it is   4 being 2gethr erth packages
our skin give off ar spreding our legs opning 2
th returning go home white blu ensirkuling th

fullest moon xchange star saphire fire

food kiss in ths plane we nevr know th last word

anee final say isint ours it all turns b4 we can say

mortal

th konstansee uv istanbul

we had driftid sew much
our boat ourselvs th oars n our lost in
tensyuns

n th sun th sun sew hot on our shouldrs
backs n our sumwhat skewd heds

how long had we driftid yet we wer cumming
closr in2 th harbour
we had playd psychik
games 2gethr n didint know aneemor if we
cud live 2gethr
we got closr 2 shore home ths
outing had prhaps got th bettr uv us eye was
passiv accepting wher he wantid mor assertif
he was 2 leedr wher i wud want him mor
egalitarian he put me on trial sew much uv th
time sew whn he sd i was dewing well i wud
try 2 repeet without knowing what aspekt uv
my behaviour he was admiring i kept saying
lets cant we remembr th warmth thats all
wayze btween us *cant we build on that*

no he sd wev dun it all now eye want yu ther
all th time 2 cum home 2 but nu guys all
nu guys 4 me allwayze wudint yu grow 2
dislike me tho i askd n i dont think i want
ths aneemor its not bad a littul uv it n sum
times maybe a 3sum eye can think uv diffrent
things various konstrukts n sumtimes feeling
th wisdom uv it but if its relentless n nothing is
4evr xsept th word 4evr
segue its enuff ther as we dockd th
boat n tuk off running 2 th alain delon

film festival   whil viewing th mooveez each
realizing theyr needs each uv n with each othr
wer kontradiktoree n drifting in2 inkompatabilitee
4 sum time now

they suddnlee lookd at each othr n realizd
it was 2 xcellent what they cud n did share held
hands kissd teering a bit droppd theyr
xklusyunaree n b attitudes n watchd evreething
all ovr agen   they had seen b4 th cumming dayze
from *purpul noon 2 monsieur klein*n sailing n
rowing at nite   undr th fullest moon theyr hearts
n groins sew full n not turning away renewd
2gethr   th konstansee uv istanbul

th origin uv missing ficksyuns th origin uv th missing dicksyuns th lettr d d d d d eeee duh d notaysyuns d vakaysyuns d salutasyuns d salinaysyuns

th dangrs uv prettee a giant appul apeerd in th sky
with a large penguin n kormorant looking as if tussul
ing ovr it whl pushing it ovr th hillee part uv th yard
off th kliff n in2 th see dont

yu know go d e e

we can nevr know who or what espeshulee
  who if ther is a who creatid us th
    poignansee uv   that sumtimes th
    tragedee uv it   whn we hurt each
    othr ovr what   **d**   we cant n dont know
    we ar an amay   zing book wch cannot
      evr know its   author or authors
    we dont have th kapabilitee 4 that de rigeur
    lets stop kidding ourselvs ooomph de finatur
    its not in us not in our design deklining
      no kapabiliteez sew far d fining d riding
    2 reelee know our origins jammd konfitur
konfined 4 enigma tho tragikalee its in us 2 keep
    trying n keep on pretending n hurt othrs 4 our
beleefs ask joan uv ark cannot we regardless
touch each othr ahhh its not eezee eye know
its in th hush aftr nite fall th loss uv th goddess
god s within us if we give 2 much ovr 2 th othr
depleysyun he sd n aneeway all th manee wayze
  we have 2 b trew with each othr n what dew we
know no mor we fly inside th kormorants beek n
eyez reside in th see n th appul n th penguins splen
did splayd feet inning uv f dee n speek looking in
2 th fire going 4 th unknown n unknowabul gods
n goddesses whispr trewths no mor theyr 2 much
trubul tho if peopul want 2 i as prplexd by th
loophole in evree thinking see above n thers no
assurans from outside if peopul want 2 b d votid

2 whatevr ium glad its theyr life n it can b interest
ing *as long as ther is th total separaysyun uv church
n state* dus theyr devosyun have 2 b accurate longs no
hurting 2 much damage arint they *no mor*   me anee
who els am i i els i cum 2 yu chemikalee prepared
brout 2 yu by love rescues us from our obdurate axes
whatevr yu beleev in th imperfekt solipsisms
at th time if yr a bit shakee with all ths its onlee
bcoz we ar shakn by th moon beems have gone we
cry out 2 them re tred our groov thredings jammd 4 th
xcellent nite hug full moon sew low n rockin evn
they wer a great group we *carree on*
yu know yr in th countree massivlee manee treez sky lu
minous lakes heer kiyots woolvs loons yu evr think as i
did wuns recentlee she sd uv kours ther is a god or god
dess plural whatevr reelee howevr th linguistik mewsik
no theokrasee intendid nun takn did we anee uv us
make all or anee uv ths no uv kours we wer creatid tho
still evolving we can get bettr mor sharing mor creativ n
how dew we find th storeez 4 anee uv ths th stores 4
ths that dont divide us in our diffrent klimate kollektivs
memorizing all th availabul texts in all th availabul
kulturs lern n unlern it all n lern n *carree on* see th
dansrs rise from th mirroring lake fire wheels they glide
with n sit n watch undr th blu spruce tree smell th pine
branches n feel n see th changing pickshurs in th fire n
heer th mewsik uv th dansrs circuling th surface uv th
lake n *carree onnn* uv th souls uv th glayzd tactile reesons
4 we can nevr reelee evn steepd in know evn sew
beautiful n uplifting oftn sew manee uv all our storeez
xplanaysyuns reveering them all n th varietee uv texts
providing sophistikatid specees narrativ base prevent us
from thinking ther is onlee wun way if we bcum familyar
love all th manee wayze help us *we can nevr know* evn
we feel th terribul loving longing 4 our creators in urban
settings hardr wer surroundid by all our own works ego
what can we know love each othr wherevr we ar weul
nevr know aneething els n carree on n rue d *carie onnn*

enchantment

'...now we can see each othr n
our mor uplifting storeez...'

-vernon richards

ahh th waves uv neglekt n lafftr th sharings uv
elektrikul sparks uv kours langwages n
self ar konstrukts konstruktid that gives us th
freedom 2 moov btween whats th
big idea n swimming in th aegean
whil thers still time

skin rubbings o his beautiful back 2 touch
n grayze my hand ovr it ovr his ass whil eye
suck his beautiful cock destineez sew
multipul n refraktiv seem 2
want 2 b satisfied
satisfying th ovr
load uv nesting washes in th
mondrian basin

th seeming horizontal
lines uv blood n vertikul desire shredding th demo
graphiks n th wrestling angels remors ovr theyr
inabiliteez 2 get things bettr yet 4 us such as an
encountr with th bad wizard or witch no mattr
evn if yu dont want 2 b welcum evreewher
yu wunt b

sum peopul harbor resentment n wait 4 yu til
yr wanting kompanee with them thn *pow*   no
mattr it will all happn n moments uv sereen
n powrful n amayzing beauteez n th time
howevr varied n bursting with whatevr wundrs n
greef 2 glow our souls lapping in th harbor lites
undr th full moon b4 we take off

thru th giant oystr petal clouds
pink n green dragons   sew epik

in sum places splendidlee
struck
                shivr in th ascending d lite

        theyr gold eyez flash
        cast brite lite ovr th tall buildings
        ships n xcitements uv us
                all   undr

in our beds dockyards n hammocks
            stir n rise n look

        out from our watree berths
            thru th fires we will all go thru

a wundrful time at last

whn we wer born a spidr hung ovr

our basinets huge at nite n onlee whn
evr no peopul wer around or visiting
with beautiful tits arms or kraydul
songs

ths huge spidr silvr n black n furree
  droppd strange n xotik liquid in2 our
mouths n opn eyez

  remembring ths is like teering opn a page
from a bound blank book reveeling sum secret
    text

my middul sistr n eye in our cribs looking
      up at   th sky th ceiling th nite
    ths spidr a reel sheherazade tons uv
      strange spookee storeez   it fed in2 us
        its manee eyez gleeming

  sumtimez it lowerd itself closr on 2 us
with its hanging crane web
          n spilld mor thn evr uv its
wet stuff in2 us

  our erth mothr wud cum in2 us n
      notising a strange smell in th room
  whats that o my deers n whats ths
strange ickee swetee stuff on my baybeez
n kiss it n towell it off us

    we wer all transforming it had bin a
                  diffikult

142

krossing our home planet prhaps named
zatria   at th time   glowing n vulnrabul
embryos hurtuling thru
goldn turbulent space

protekt th gift protekt th gift she was
singing in th far futur th beautiful poet by
th sacrid grass dunes shediak nouveau
brunswick   from heer yu cud see
l'isle de prins eduard yu cud maybe swim
2 it sumwun cud n th long black fetherd
birds swooping ovr th

doreez cumming in from th see

that was all 2 cum n go lustrous in
our psychik dreem space

heer my sistr n me
in our beds   twins almost
at timez   tumbuld down in our duvets n
covrlets
keeping th spidr kompanee
nite aftr nite day aftr day
whnevr tall peopul
wer not around

th storeez th huge spidr wud tell us   in
sinuating whispring in2 our tiny ears

what it boils down 2   finalee
a lone figur   mooving thru th
landscape looking 2 konnekt
thru valleez uv perls weeping
cutting feet   on sharp blood banks
th terror uv th proprtee   n its spells
uv proteksyun from each othr

soothing reptiles in our brains
limbs loins sorrows   loves touching
each strand uv watr rushing on2 with
our kisses minds
imaginaysyuns
tumbuling maps uv wher we can nevr go
until we dew all th plesyurs
technikolour ekstaseez

th spidr pours all ths
in2 us until we almost burst
cry gurgul
take our stride thru th snow mountins
2 leen on nothing we separate sew long
we think we ar separate
dailee revolushyuns molekularlee
minutelee uv milisecondlee uv th dna

papr drilling thru th moistyur drowning

esophogus timbre heer th mewsik uv th
treez sweeping thru th desert th oxygen
fire n what we put in2 our mouths   yell
lasting 4 all times

we get it th huge spidr eezes pushes
off 2 othrs
2 th embroild cares skraping
klay n burnt bones
it cums from sets out
agen aftr drinking 2 manee
memoreez   it can hurt

watch n with sew manee figurs
uv konsciousness let go th long
breething processes uv splitting
dividing faltring heeling n dispersing
agen